A Self-Help Book for People Who Don't Like Self-Help Books!

DOC SAVAGE

The Reading Glass Books
(888) 420-3050
www.readingglassbooks.com
production@readingglassbooks.com

Table of Contents

Dedication to Dr. Tracy who taught me all I know about psychology! My children who teach me humility. My husband Matt who never dulls my sparkle. To my family and friends who tolerate and support my many hobbies!

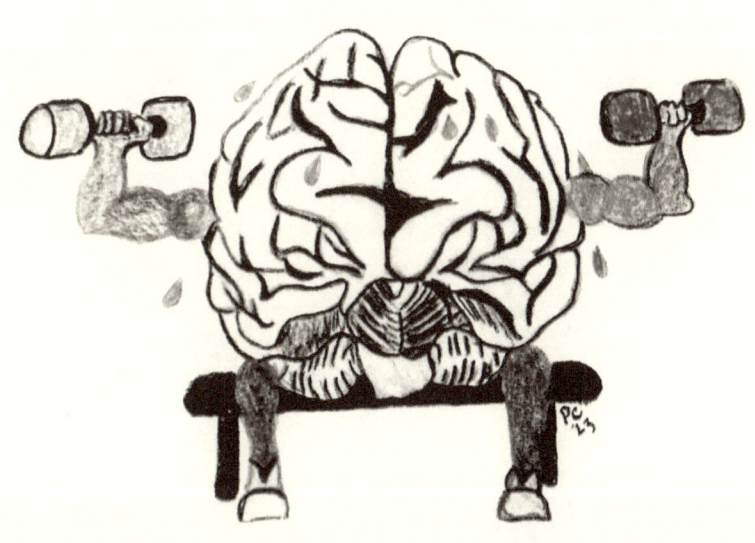

CHAPTER 1

You're perfect so why change...

Change is one of those tricky items. We love it and we hate it. Sometimes at the exact same time which is even harder to wrap our mind around. In this self-help book for people who don't like self-help books I will explain some basics. One of the basics is how change occurs within ourselves. We are all creatures of habit and past behavior is the best predictor of future behavior. So... if that is true, what's the point of reading this book any further? Well... negative voice in my head, thank you for asking at such a perfect moment. Change is like your favorite food.

It requires two ingredients at the same time baked over a minimum of a two-week time frame (some critics argue up to 21 days). These two ingredients are:

1.) Motivation = a desire for a specific outcome.

2.) Insight = the ability to look at your own behavior and identify errors in thinking and your actions. Number one is where most people begin and typically never make it through number two.

"Why?" you ask... Well, great question. Because it sucks. It's exhausting to look at our thoughts and our behaviors and identify what we are doing right and wrong.

Oftentimes it's much easier to be motivated and find a reason that our idea or plan won't work. It's also very easy to blame something or someone else on our inability to follow through. I'm too busy to work out, I don't have time, my family doesn't support me.

We all do it at different times to different degrees. It is a natural part of being human, but it does not help us achieve the things we want in life. Pointing out the faults in others does not decrease our faults, it just shifts the spotlight for a few minutes. We all return back to our own self at some point and we are left with sitting in our own minds and bodies.

Well my friend, if you are ready for change, then "LET'S GET READY TO RUMBLE!"

1.) A very popular model of change is from Prochaska. He talked about cycles of change and refers to it as a pie where people move from one slice to the next. Let's examine – What stage are you in?

    a. Precontemplation – Others indicate that you should change, although you don't agree or at least fully agree. For example, your doctor says that you're pre-diabetic and you need to change your eating style and you tell yourself that doctors just say that crap to bill insurance. Now, of course, deep down you know that doctor is right and you secretly wonder what took him/her so long to say that.

    b. Contemplation – You are getting annoyed with those people and their opinions, but maybe it would be beneficial to think about what that change might look like. This is the part where you wonder what it would be like to be a type 2 diabetic. This is where we allow fear to creep in, fear that maybe these others are right. We start to wonder what it would be like to make the change that others are suggesting. Like, how will it look to eat healthy? What sacrifices do I have to make, what foods do I have to cut out? Do I have to exercise? Blaa gross! Only crazy people exercise. I'm not going to get a matching velvet tracksuit. I mean it! But, what would it feel like to fit better in my pants? I wonder what it would be like to have more energy and not get winded climbing up steps. Hmm, maybe I would benefit from changing.

c. Preparation – Getting everything in order for that upcoming change. You have decided that change will benefit you. Nobody reaches their best version of themselves by being stagnant. Here is where all the planning comes into place. While studying group dynamics in graduate school one study talked about how weight watchers is the most successful diet modification. It stated that because it was socially based and that since you were held accountable by getting on the scale in front of someone else that it motivates people at a higher level. For most of us, when we move into the preparation phase we announce to others that we will be making some changes. It could be, "I'm going to quit smoking" or "I'm going to start a new career." If you decided to change your diet, this is where you cave and buy that amazing 1980's tracksuit with the lightning bolt of yellow or hot pink across your chest and down the leg. This is a good way to let everyone on your block know that you are prepared for that awesome change coming up.

d. Action – Here goes the cheer – "We want action action action, A-C-T --- (pause) --- I-O-N ACTION Boys ACTION WOOOH!! (envision kicks and fist pumps and vigorous enthusiasm all over the place). During this phase we go ahead and follow through with the plans we set up in the last phase. This one sucks. "It's Hard!!!" (picture a four year old stomping on the ground and throwing their fists to their sides). Yup boys and girls, this one is hard. But anything worth doing, like picking yourself up and making it happen... is worth the extra effort. During this phase, especially for 'BAD' habits, it's best to add safe-guards and ways to catch yourself....... Add ways to be accountable to yourself and others. This could be like taking pictures of yourself in that sexy ass tracksuit day one and once a week each following week. It could be buying a matching tracksuit for your best friend to wear when you force each other to the gym when you're 'just not feeling it.' (Which, let's be honest will probably never happen, who 'likes' working out? Only crazy people, we already established this one.) The biggest trick to this phase is making it into a habit that can be a part of your every day or week. If you can do it consistently for 14-21 days, bam… you've successfully made it a habit. Pfew, those 21 days felt like a few years, but here I am making that awesome change.

e. Maintenance – Wohoo! Way to go Negative Nancy or Debbie Downer. You got through the hardest part and now it's streamlined. This phase comes into play in one of two ways. Either Action has been established for two to three weeks or you found your consistent method that has worked well for those few weeks. One of the other tricks to successful behavior change from Shawn Achor is to make the activity one that can be within 20 seconds from you. He says that if you want to play the guitar it needs to be within 20 seconds of where you spend most of your time. If you want to watch less TV then put the remote 20 seconds away from the TV. Maintenance is about finding ways to make these changes stay and repel the bad behaviors from returning. 'Be gone evil spirits' (in Dana Carvy's church lady voice).

f. Relapse – We don't like this phase, but we are all human and we will fall down frequently. Batman provides a great reframe. When Bruce's dad comes down the well and says, "Why do we fall Bruce? So we can learn to pick ourselves back up again." That's what this phase is all about. This area is where insight is very important, we may need to become detectives in our own lives and do a little investigative research. If and when we relapse it's most important to activate that difficult thing called insight and reflect on what we are thinking and doing that is preventing our success.

2.) Smoking Cessation – Change occurs in layers. This aspect is about understanding more about our own excuses for change, our resistance to make modifications. We have a tendency to say... "I already tried buying a tracksuit, it makes too much noise. I couldn't work out in it." Maybe the tracksuit didn't work when you tried it the first time in 1988, but maybe in 2018 it's ready for a come-back (we know you couldn't throw it out even though you only wore it once).

During one of the studies on smoking cessation (because quitting smoking is one of the hardest things to do chemically speaking), they found out that on average (remember there are people with less and more times) people quit smoking eight times before they found what worked and successfully quit. What was even more interesting was that what finally did the trick, whether it be – going cold turkey – using the patches – the gum – hypnosis (etc.) (When it stuck) was a method they had tried before. So, maybe you tried chewing on toothpicks the second time you quit and it didn't work, but the eighth time it did work. Smart people, oh, I mean researchers, argue that change occurs in layers and we need those 'trial and errors' to understand what works best for ourselves. Remember what works for most will not work for all.

This concept means that maybe the 'Snicker diet' didn't work before when you tried to lose weight but combined with your new knowledge and experience if you combine high protein with Snickers and exercise twice a week, you will see results. (Please don't try anything as obscure as the Snicker diet... somethings are exactly how they appear = Too good to be true). This also means that it's important for you to stay patient with yourself and explore the ways that you respond best to change and what keeps you on that path.

Change happens in layers. As we learn more about ourselves, we start to develop ways that work and ways that fit us. Each of us are not cookie-cutters. One size does not fit all and we need to find out what works best for us. This will require some give and take.

3.) Wagon Wheel of Life Stressors/Contributors.

    a. This is another way to visualize your life. The items that affect you as a person or cause stress go into the wagon wheel. Each aspect covers a 'spoke'. Remember that not all spokes are equal, some become damaged or stressed at different times. The ways to visualize are the spoke being mild strength (which means it was damaged) moderate, then heavy strength. This is a nice way to view these sections of your life and see what needs to be addressed.

    i.   There are two ways to approach this. Start with the most compromised section and work on that one. Or work on one that is only moderately affected and strengthen that one. If too many of the spokes become damaged then the wheel will not turn. It will crush under its own weight (yes that is a parallel to emotions like stress/anxiety or depression).

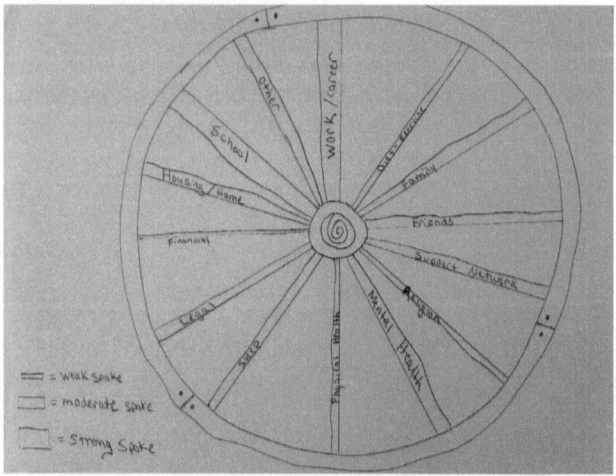

    ii.

    iii.   It can be useful to take a look at goals after you assess strengths/weaknesses. Feel free to add anything that is missing for your own life to the wheel.

4.) Energy – Where is your energy going and why?

    a.   I find this the most interesting way to reassess ourselves. What are you spending your time and energy on each day? Is it negative or positive? Maybe it's even neutral. Here is a way to better assess that question.

    b.   Write down all the people and things that you think about on a daily basis. Then place yourself in the middle. Go through the list and establish whether the energy is; mild, moderate, or heavy. Then place a positive or negative next to that energy. If it is negative energy then it gets a (minus). If it's positive then it gets a (plus). You can send out positive energy and receive negative. There are no rules with that.

c.   After you finish the circle, total up the numbers for each person or thing. Remember that negative energy is always a minus and positive energy is a plus.

d.   After that is done, tally up all of the pluses and minuses. The goal of this is for your number to be zero. Zero would signify that you put out in the world what you get back. That you view each of your interactions as worthwhile and fulfilling. You are not taking more than you are giving. Remember that this is subjective and when we look inward there is always some room for error but also improvement.

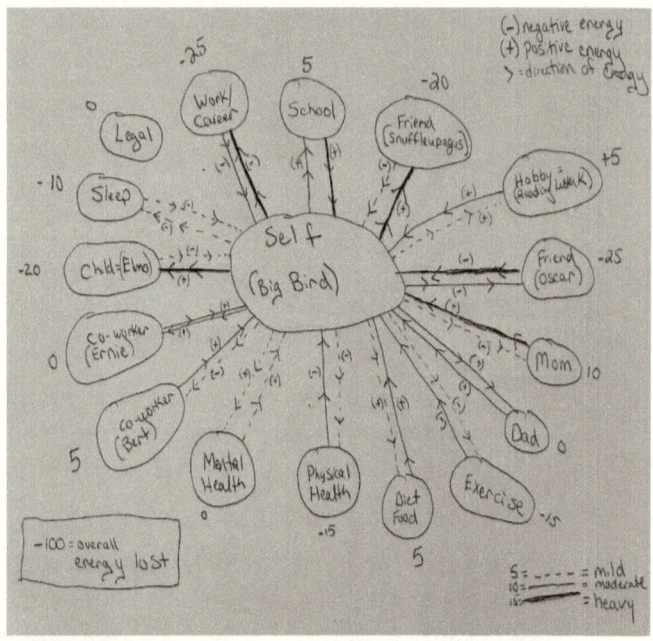

1.)

2.) If we examine this example we see a few things. Let's start with the center. I made the person Big Bird, but really this should be you. So typically you would put your own name in the middle or say, "Me."

3.) Each of the bubbles/circles surrounding 'me' is something that you spend time or energy on. This does include things that consume mental energy. Some of these things can be bad. Like the example of the friend Oscar. He's really a grouchy old man, he takes up a lot of mental space. We think a good deal about him (moderate energy). It is all negative because he really bothers us. What we get back is heavy negative. He calls you with all his problems, he never listens to you or tries to help you. He sends sarcastic messages all day, he's just a drain on your energy. So, he's a negative with heavy energy. This means that he is an overall negative energy. Remember, negative energy always takes away from the quality of your life, so negatives add up, leaving Oscar as a friend as a negative 25 on the energy. Let's explain: you give -10, this means that you may think about him often and feel mad about the way he takes your energy, you may even be mad that you are still friends with him. He gives you -15. He is always complaining. You are never there for him enough. He's quick to be critical of you. This is a way to organize your thoughts into these energy numbers.

4.) Mom is an interesting energy. She gives you positive heavy (+15) and you give her negative mild energy (-5), it's partially because you just feel exhausted by the time mom calls and then you feel negative later on that you weren't more helpful or supportive. So instead of more positive you are only positive +10. But remember, the goal is to be zero so being plus 10 means that someone is giving in more than you are contributing. In this example, it's your mother.

5.) Healthiest relationships will be a zero, then a low positive to a higher positive than the negatives. If we look at the chart above:

a. The best are: Dad – Co-worker (Ernie) – Mental Health & Legal (notice legal has no energy out or in. This is reserved for things that are out on the periphery, but maybe don't take any energy right now. They may possibly come into the circle shortly.

b. The next best are: School – Hobby (reading the letter K) – Diet/food – Co-worker (Bert)

c. Then: Mom & Sleep

d. Next is: Sleep – Exercise – Physical Health - Friend (Snuffleupagus) – Child/son (Elmo) –

e. Last is: Work – Friend (Oscar)

f. We add up each section, remember negative energy adds up, while positive energy can be exchanged. As we add up each component, we get a grand total of = negative 100 energy

g. This example means that we lose out on 100 energy regularly with our current system. Of course hitting a zero is the goal, but unlikely without being aware and focusing on the energy you distribute. If you fill out this form and you come out ahead by under 50 then you are on the right track to zero.

h. Remember that the goal is zero. We want to give positive, eliminate the negative people or things in our life and focus on balance.

i. If I looked at this cycle as your therapist I would focus on a few things, Oscar, work, and mom. Oscar and work either need less energy or to look at ways to replace them or give them less energy. In reference to mom, I would figure out how to give her positive energy so that we can quickly balance that relationship out more.

j. Lastly, 0 is the goal, but 5's and 10's are on the right track. If we look at Elmo, our child, he's 1 year old. We give high positive and get crying and fussy back, but remember, as time goes on this relationship will balance itself out more.

k.   I often look at 25's, 20's, & 15's (positive or negative) and see if there's a way to start reorganizing to gain a sense of control. Remember, you are in control of your energy. You choose what you focus on and what surrounds you. There will be times in your life that you feel more in control and others where you feel like things are happening 'to you.' This is a great time to take a fresh set of eyes on this energy cycle.

l.   Lastly, I would encourage you to complete an energy cycle today (a quick one takes about 10-15 minutes). It's a quick 'temperature' on your life and energy. In three months, I would do it again. It's a great way to see where you are and where you are headed.

e.   Here's another tool for assessing negative energy – take a person or situation who has been bothering you. Take an hour, write down on a paper (usually tick marks) on how often this person or situation enters your mind. Add it up (over the course of an hour) how many times you think about that person or event. This could even be used with traumatic events. Not future events, but past events.

Figure out what percentage of time is used on this 'thing.' Let's say you spend 10 minutes an hour on this thing. If we did the math we would divide 10 by 60 and get 1/6th or .16 percent. So, if that is 16 we would then multiply it by the number of hours that you are awake. Let's say (if we all get enough sleep, yeah right) that you are awake for 15 hours a day. That means that we would multiply 16 times 15 hours of wakefulness. The total is 240. So just for fun let's convert that to dollars.

Now I want you to take $240 dollars (by the way that is a lot of money in one day) and either send it to me or throw it out the window. If the idea of giving me or throwing $240 dollars out the window bothers you, then you need to make a change. Your energy and mental space are worth more than any amount of money. Please stop throwing away your precious money/energy.

    i.   Now comes the critical question, is this how you want to continue spending your time/money? Remember your energy is precious and only you can choose what you focus on and 'spend your money on'.

CHAPTER 2

Wait, Perfect doesn't exist?

1.) This is a special message to my type A people. Those who strive for the immaculate. Now, you may be type A because you are hungry for success. You may strive for perfection because you fear not measuring up to others. I mean if you're perfect then nobody can say shit to you. Here's the reason why I'm only going to edit this book twice. If you give into that need for 'error proof' then you continue to feed that anxiety. You give into that insatiable monster and then you must keep feeding it. There is no liquid diet or restricted intake, only more is allowed. The challenge with this framework is that if everything has to be 'wonderful', soon the entire world becomes overwhelming.

For example, I can't have friends over until I make my house look amazing. "Things must be in order" tends to yield a reason you don't socialize or do harder things. Here is the news flash... Humans are imperfect creatures. They are not symmetrical, for example people have a dominant hand (or preference). This also helps alert us that we will not do things the same or 'right' every time. This is why athlete's practice constantly. Because their performance will not be the same every time, even in similar situations. Even statistically the absolute best number (which is extremely rare and very unlikely) is 99.9%. In human behavior there is no such thing as 100%. Experiencing 100% on any activity is just as likely as having Bigfoot join the NBA to start his own shoe line.

2.) Scientists that study human behavior had to create a scale to represent those kooky humans by creating not a linear graph, but rather one that is referred to as the bell curve.

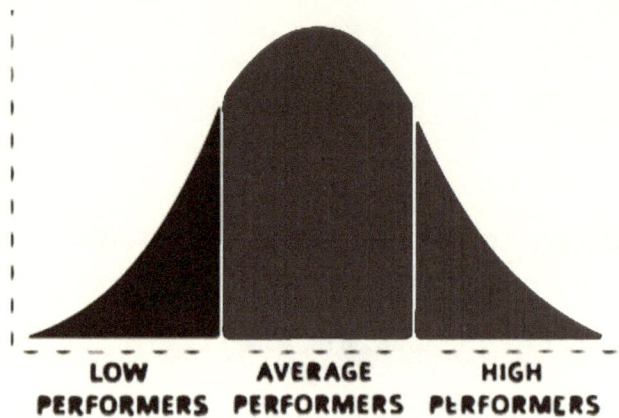

LOW PERFORMERS   **AVERAGE PERFORMERS**   **HIGH PERFORMERS**

a.

b. As you can see. It looks like a bell. The most common human behavior is in the middle. That's where the 'majority' rests. Maybe think of the line in the middle as the average speed limit. It's the area, in this case the speed, in which the bulk of the population behave.

c. Then on the left side will be those people that are slower than the speed limit. These people are going under because they may have car trouble, dangerous or unsafe roads, a difficult time texting and driving, or they may be trying to grab something from their kids in the back seat. But for whatever reason, they are under the speed limit.

d. Then you will have people on the right side. These people are in a hurry to get things done, maybe they realized that they left their stove on and need to rush home, or their destination is more important than yours, or maybe they just disagree with the posted speed limit. Whatever the reason they are above the curve which becomes less common the higher the speed.

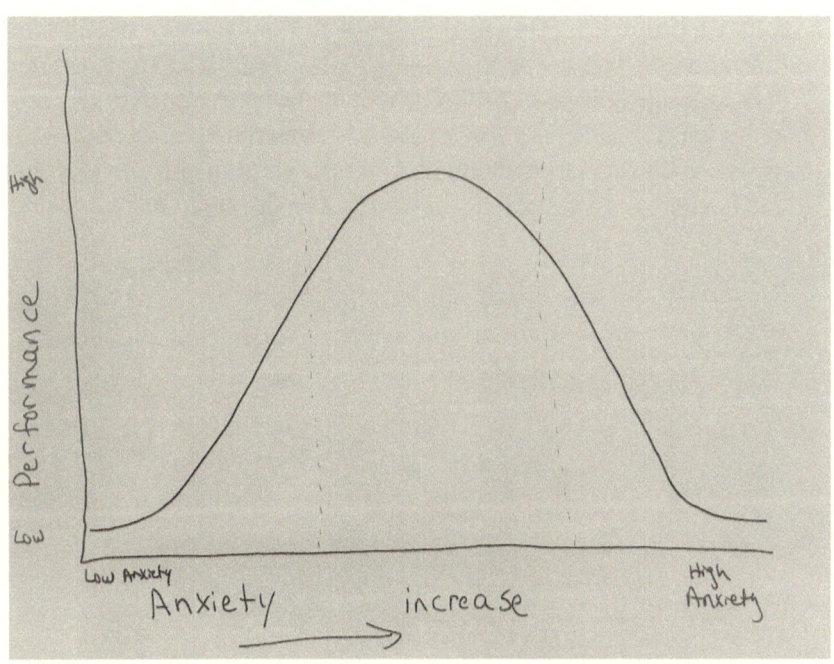

This visual helps us understand test performance as it correlates with anxiety.

3.) As we see, when anxiety is low (i.e., you don't care or don't want to be bothered) then your performance is low. On the flip side, if your anxiety is high then your performance is also low. The idea is that we need a moderate level of anxiety for optimal performance.

4.) Of course as in all behavior there are different motivations. Another reason people strive for the perfect 'holy grail' is not really about being perfect, but about moving away from negativity. People who strive for perfection tend to hate criticism, and this is a way to prevent it. "If I can just do everything right then nobody can say anything bad about me." Yikes... no pressure.

5.) Now that we have clarified the imaginary nature of 'perfection' we will address the last undiscussed motivation for perfection. Due to the fact that perfection does not exist the person knows that what they strive towards will not happen, which becomes a negative self-fulfilling prophecy. This way they prove to themselves that they are 'not enough.' It is a way to continue hateful self-talk. For example: "See you always mess up," "Why did you even try for that job, you knew you were never going to get it," "Why did you say that, now everyone thinks that you're dumb." This train of thought is unforgiving and harsh, but it does not move you into a healthy mental framework.

CHAPTER 3

Now that we know we can't be perfect, let's set some attainable goals – reach out for human perfection.

1.) Whenever I start a session, I have people write down a minimum of five goals for themselves. This is a great way to start self-reflection. Start with five goals, but these goals require some specific details. A goal needs to be written as an affirmation. What the heck is an affir..mation? Well, what a great question. An affirmation is making a statement positive. An example would be, "I want to stop negative self-talk." If we break down that statement, we see two negatives (stop and negative). The brain has a way of ignoring words following a negative word. So, the brain hears nothing after "stop." The best way to get the brain to comply, which will lead to behavioral modifications is to say nice things. Think about this for a second, if someone says something mean to you, you are less likely to want to help them, but if you hear positive statements then it's easier to feel motivated.

   a. Let's try. "The report you wrote was sloppy and disorganized, you need to try harder." Notice your thoughts/feelings.

   b. Now: " The report you wrote was creative and intriguing." Notice your thoughts/feelings.

   c. I'm guessing that you enjoyed the second one more, but you will probably spend more energy fixating on the first one. (We will cover the neurological reason for this later).

   d. The way that we would 're-frame' the original statement (I want to stop negative self-talk). First we drop all negative statements. Then find a positive way to state our goal. Then state things in a way that is attainable.

e. Last, make sure that it's measurable.

   i. 1st rule = drop negative statements: I want self-talk

   ii. 2nd rule = find a positive way to state it: I want positive self-talk

   iii. 3rd rule = state it in a way that is attainable: I want to give myself compliments when I do small successful things throughout the day. (OR) I want to say something nice to myself every hour.

   iv. 4th rule = make sure that the goal is a statement: I want to give myself one compliment an hour for the next four weeks. (OR) I want to monitor my thinking and replace negativity with statements of affection every day for the next 14 days.

2.) STOVE TOP METHOD = As we move away from perfection we now focus on those pesky attainable goals during our everyday life. These are things that we can achieve in one day. These items should take approximately one hour or less to complete. There are a few phases of this model. We call this the Stove Top Method. In phase 1 we focus on only completing four tasks a day. Keep in mind that these tasks can only take up to one hour to complete. For example, if you say that one of your four tasks is going to be cleaning. Then the task needs to be clarified and isolated to last only one hour. Cleaning can be a very long and daunting task. This means that we choose chores that would only take an hour or add up to an hour. For example, cleaning the toilet = 10 min / cleaning the counter (depends on how cluttered it is) = 10-20 min / scrub the sink = 10 min / scrub the tub/shower 20 min / wash the floor = 10 min. Those tasks equal about an hour.

   a. If we try another chore we may say "do laundry" this task is guaranteed to take more than an hour but it is broken up. (Unless you are 'Little House on the Prairie' and hand wash all your clothes.)

   b. Remember the purpose of this exercise is to increase feelings of success and completion. Often those that are 'perfectionists' will have 15 emergent items on their daily 'to do' list. We all know that all of those items are not going to be completed. In the rare case all 15 are completed, it will not be to the high standard that is 'expected.'

c.   One of the things that happens with those that suffer from 'perfectionism' is a sense that they didn't do 'enough.' This unrealistic list full-fills their fears that they 'aren't enough' or didn't do enough. This will just continue the negative cycle of feeling inadequate.

d.   Everyone has their own political views on president Clinton, but despite those arguments most would agree that he was a 'successful' president. He was asked, "How were you so successful as a president?" He said, "I did four things a day, that was it." I think there is something to be gained from his statement. We all get bogged down with thinking that we must or need to get so much accomplished and sometimes it's just as simple as four things. We have all heard the statement, "the pyramids were not built in a day". This is a solid statement. During the Chicago marathon I saw someone with a sign, "It took the Cubs 108 years to win the series, go at your own pace." It was solid advice. We need to follow our own path and find our pace. Four items a day is feasible and healthy. We can adjust from there.

e.   If we look at the top of a stove we have 4 burners. If we put two big pots in the back, that way we can slowly warm things up and we can put many items on the 'back burner'. We want to put the hot items in the front. If you think about it, we need to keep our eye on the front burners, so the items in there are important.

f.   If you are someone that does too many things or over-prioritize too many things then nothing can be a priority. On top of it, you probably start to feel a bit crazy by all the things you 'can't finish.' That is not good for motivation or someone's psyche.

g.   This first phase of stovetop is to get you to prioritize only four things. Yes, you read that correctly, only four things. I believe in you. Only four things. They can't be more than an hour. Then you can sit back on your couch and go, 'ahh, this is what it feels like to be a winner.'

h.   Use the image and make a copy or re-create it. Start writing things in daily. You can even get a dry erase board and update it daily/weekly.

Image by Richard Heger

3.) Stove top – phase 2

a.   Remember that Phase 2 is only for those that have mastered phase one. The hardest thing is to move success from a huge list into four items. As we develop this list it moves into four specific items.

b.   Those four items are (1) work/school (2) Personal (3) Social (4) tertiary hygiene

  i.   1) The first item is work/school. In this you are allowed to complete a task for up to one hour for work or school that will make tomorrow less stressful. It could be preparing a lecture or anything that will help the next day be more successful. Maybe starting early on an essay. Getting a head start on a reading assignment.

ii. The second item is 'personal,' this item is about doing one thing for yourself. People that are perfectionistic tend to neglect themselves or their own needs. During this section it is important to do something that you like. This could be reading a book, taking a bath, going to the gym, painting. It could even be masturbating. In this area it is whatever you need to do to feel like you are taking care of yourself.

iii. The third item is 'Social." In this section you are required to reach out to someone else. You are only allowed your most frequent contact to count for three times of the week. For example, if you live with your mom, dinner with her can only count for up to three times a week. If you have a spouse they can only count for three times a week. This means that you have to reach out to other friends or family or coworkers the other days. In this section it can be a phone call in the car for five to ten minutes. This area is meant for you to reach out to others and create a strong social bond with others. (Facebook or social media does NOT count). It must be a phone call or special time spent with that person.

iv. The last item is called 'tertiary hygiene.' This item is intended to cover things that need to be addressed the day before. This is something that will make the next day more productive. The definition of hygiene is a series of practices performed to preserve health and prevent illness. We use the word tertiary because these are not the first or second items that we tend to think about, these are the items that are frequently forgotten.

1.) If I suggested that we go camping, what would you bring? A primary item would be a tent, a sleeping bag, food, water, and a heat source. A secondary item would be a way to cook the food, pots pans, a flashlight, and of course bug spray. A tertiary item would be garbage bags, napkins, toilet paper, and extra batteries. If you forget those things it can be a very unpleasant experience (provided that you like camping to begin with).

2.) The assessment for your tertiary hygiene items looks like this, "What do I need to complete or check for today so tomorrow is smooth?"

- Common items are making sure that you have enough clean socks or underwear, having toilet paper, fuel, or milk. Renewing your driver's license or bus pass (events that only happen annually or infrequently). Getting your oil changed or tires checked. Paying a ticket on time. Even though these items are small, they will cause a large strain and stress to your day, a strain that was preventable through this checklist. Think of the last time you ran out of clean socks, it probably threw you off your morning schedule enough to cause you to be late or at least start the day frustrated. Make sure to put things in your #4 section that will help your next day be more successful.

v. There is one more concept that you can add to this model which is reserved for the rarest of moments. This was provided by a client. The method is called "Microwave Method" This is when we keep all the traditional stovetop concepts, but rather have the microwave for last minute emergencies. It wouldn't be used often, but sometimes we need to 'nuke' something quickly. The "microwave method tends to be applied more to last minute emergencies or business models.

4.) Behavior change – 20 second rule. Shawn Achor is a positive psychologist who studies how to increase success. In his book "The Happiness Advantage" he talks about tricks that help us change and sustain our behavior.

a. I've worked with clients from all ages. I've had some people in their later years and some of them have asked me, "Am I too old, is there any hope for me to get better?" I explain to them the two things that are required for change to occur (which we already covered). 1) Insight and 2) is motivation. Think about a diet that you tried and failed. You likely had the motivation for this diet change, but if you didn't have insight into why you are behaving that way or for that matter 'Not doing' what you need to do, then the behavior change will only last until the motivation runs out. It will not be sustainable.

b. Shawn talks about the 20 second rule. He states that any 'new' desired behavior is more attainable if the object is 20 seconds from you. He gives an excellent personal account of how he tried to learn the guitar and made very 'unrealistic' goals of practicing. After three weeks he was grossly below his objective. He then worked on insight. He noticed that he was more 'comfortable' sitting on the couch and grabbing the remote. So, he took the remote and walked it 20 seconds away from the couch and moved the guitar next to the couch. Within a few weeks he had hit his goal and was practicing guitar more than he had originally planned. Motivation is important, but without insight it has a greater likelihood of making us feel defeated or like 'failures.' Even when we have the best of intentions.

CHAPTER 4

I'm stuck on my imperfection…. Let's lipo that trauma out of your brain, "Nurse hand me the suction"

Wouldn't that be nice? Every time you focus on what you did or how you messed up or even recalling that 'horrible' past experience that we could go in and ablate it, or take white-out to that neurotransmitter and block it. I recall a story about my grandfather. After he passed my cousin got his van. My cousin said that when he got the van and started driving he noticed black electrical tape all over the dashboard. Each piece was in a different place and different sizes. My cousin started to remove each piece and discovered that each piece was covering up a check engine light that was illuminated. He said that everything but the 'check gas' light was lit. While on initial inspection everything 'checks out' and looks good. The problem is that underneath there are a whole host of problems. We are all guilty of this 'cover up' behavior from time to time. Each problem has a time-line of 'available neglect' until it 'stalls the car.'

1.) Realistic expectations – well what the heck is that? I now must be logical about my goals, well that's no fun. I prefer to create unattainable goals so I can remind myself of my failures at every turn. What fun is there in feeling positive and accomplished?

This is a fun section about developing attainable goals. The interesting part here is mostly due to preference. Goals are about preference. While on this topic I highly recommend small and manageable goals. Take your goal and cut it in half and if you're very perfectionistic then cut that in half again… Then and only then are you likely to be in an attainable goal. Double the time you expected to reach the goal and now you've found the right math equation.

2.) When people are in pain it can feel insurmountable. The pain can feel so overwhelming that we don't see a way out, but this is usually when we are in the middle of an emotion. Remember a key fact: Every emotion has a beginning, a middle, and an end. The middle sucks and often feels as if it's never going away. And if we've learned anything from Guns and Roses, "Nothing lasts forever, even cold November rain."

    a. Now that we know that discomfort or pain or emotions can't last forever, I want to provide a few more guidelines. Remember that these are parameters to help you gauge your own progress. If you find yourself outside of these parameters, then it is likely that you need to seek additional medical help and attention.

    b. Once a major life event takes place, there are two shifts that occur. The first two weeks are the heaviest and are often precursors to parts of the first six months. After six months we shift into a pattern and a type of homeostasis (new normal). At the two year mark we will experience another shift and for some, more of a final shift. This change at two years tends to catch people off balance. Your reaction to the first six months will repeat themselves at the two year marker. Keep in mind that this is completely 'normal' (I don't really believe that normal exists, but you get the picture.)

    c. I hear questions buzzing around. What is considered a major life event? Well, gee, thanks for asking,

        i. My magic therapy answer is 'whatever you think' but in the case you find that too ambiguous you can use this guideline.

        ii. Births, deaths, marriages, divorces, job changes, moves, deployments, returns from deployment, loss of home (fire/hurricane) and major illnesses.

        iii. Think of a new job. It's likely that you're nervous and excited at the beginning, pressure to perform and make a good impression which is highest during the first two weeks, then still present for the next six months at a slightly lower volume. At two years you may find yourself anxious again, similarly to when you started. You may find yourself comparing your performance to others, worrying about stability, promotions and longevity. If you're newly married you may find yourself wondering if you made a good decision. This sure is feeling like a forever decision (the new smell has worn off).

3.) Here we will lightly brush on trauma with the purpose to emphasize resiliency. Another book will follow which spends a greater amount of time discussing trauma and helping you develop methods to overcome that trauma. Let us spend a few minutes on understanding trauma. In its most basic definition trauma is when an intended event gets stuck or doesn't come to completion. Its definition is very simplistic, and one could easily say that the most basic event that didn't occur is traumatic. In this definition one would be correct, and everything is a trauma. Let's expand on this concept. There are two areas that expand the value 1) depth of the trauma 2) personal areas affected. We have so many different personal aspects of our life. For example, health, legal, work, school, financial, social, family, friends, etc. When we look at trauma, the 'level' of trauma rests in the number of areas that are affected by the 'stuck event' or trauma compounded by the depth/severity.

   a. On a small trauma scale let's make up a scenario. This morning when you got up you dreamed about bacon. You may have imagined the crisp smoky taste. You could picture your arteries gleefully clogging to these delicious, saturated fats. When you went to the kitchen to make breakfast you discovered that you ran out of bacon. Yes, I understand that it's hard to imagine a traumatic event more severe, but they exist. This is traumatic (in the most basic definition). An intended event (eating bacon) did not happen. If we look at the depth it is minor, you can still eat, just not the desired item. The aspects /areas are minimal (hard to really pick one outside of comfort). This event alone does not have the power of influence to affect more areas of your life than the momentary comfort. Not having bacon (which may emotionally feel heavy) will not affect any other sections of your life. You will keep your job, continue with the friendships that you have etc.

When you realize that your intended event will not occur you can experience a whole range of emotions. You may become angry blaming others for eating your bacon (even if you live alone). You might blame yourself for eating it all yesterday and not restocking the item. In your anger you may declare that the whole day is ruined and that it's 'doomed.' Your next action may be to reframe. You may say to yourself, "Well self, maybe we didn't need the extra fats," or "Maybe it's time I try the turkey bacon in the freezer," or maybe even decide to go out for breakfast with a friend you haven't seen in a while. In any case there are a host of potential responses.

    i.   In these potential responses I want you to examine which one you gravitate to the most. Is your anger turned in more frequently or out towards others? When you turn that frustration inwards, does there tend to be a lot of negative self-talk? When the response is turned outward there is a greater sense of feeling powerless to events in your life. You may notice these as patterns.

    ii.   The next important section to hone in on is what you do next to 'drive on' or 'move forward.' Do you declare the entire day a loss, do you brood over it for the next hour? Do you call others or post it so you can vent about your frustrations? Or do you choose to view this event as an opportunity? A way to change the course of the day in a potentially helpful and possibly even fun direction? This is where the opportunity for resiliency rears its head. We can become stronger with each challenge or interaction or we can become weaker. The choice is yours.

  b. It's time for a big trauma example so we can better compare. Let's say that you get into a car accident on your way to work. Your car is undrivable. In this example we have several courses of action. We can decide that the accident is the worst event ever in our lives. We can focus on all the items that we have lost, our vehicle, maybe even our job, and next comes the mental snowballs of horror. The fear of continued loss can cascade into more anxiety and depression. You may find yourself blaming others, yourself, or maybe even your vehicle or the people that designed the intersection.

i.   Remember that after each traumatic event we need to think 1) Depth/severity 2) Areas of impact / aspects affected. In the car accident example it depends on the severity of the accident. Let's say the car is totaled and there is minor physical injury to you and the two passengers in the other car. Based on that, the depth is moderate and the areas are: transportation, medical, legal, financial, possible future work/attendance. It may have a cascade of events with legal and recovery or physical therapy. It may affect your driving record or if it was someone else it may put you in a position of feeling helpless and fearful. There may be some residual fears of being in cars and feeling safe.

ii. In this next section we explore many different areas of your life affected by this stuck event. How quickly you move through each of those items will usually indicate the length of healing time that you will need emotionally. I would encourage you to write down each aspect that is affected. Then develop a plan to manage or address each of those items.

   A.   Example of a way you could organize your areas/ aspects

      a.   Legal- contact lawyer – get consultation

      b.   Legal – talk to insurance company to determine additional information required

      c.   Medical – follow up with doctor on future treatment

   d. Medical – attend all of my physical therapy appointments

   e. Financial – examine savings/ do I need a loan/ what are options

   f. Financial – how long will it take me to financially recover (create timeline)

   g. Work – talk to people about getting rides to work until I can get my car fixed / take uber/public transportation

   h. Health – spend more time at the gym to improve overall wellness. Get back to pre-injury status

   i. Health – schedule time to talk to therapist about fear of driving

4.) The more creative you are, the better you are for survival. One of the leading researchers on trauma is Bessel Van Der Kolk. He runs the trauma center out of Boston. During one of his lectures and in his book is a story of a child and trauma. It was related to a child at about the age of five that saw people jumping out of a burning building. He asked the children to draw a picture of what they saw. The little boy drew a picture of the building on fire with a big black circle on the page (this story is accessible in his book, The Body Keeps the Score). When the child was asked what the black circle represents the child said, "A trampoline so the people jumping have a place to land." There were no survivors from the fire or the people falling out of the building, but this was the child's way out of the situation. This was his way of being creative to make a new ending. This is how true resiliency works. When we can see an alternative ending through a horrible situation.

   a. I encourage you to tap into your creative side more often. The harshness of reality will always be present, but the silver lining is not obvious. It takes far more energy to be positive and optimistic, but it has more of a 'bang for your buck.' Remember your brain is naturally drawn to the negative, it is up to you to fight the 'low hanging fruit' and do something difficult. Be creative and be positive.

b. In the book, "The Art of Love" by Erich Fromm he talks about humans and their creativity. During the time when Freud was gaining traction, he had a counterpoint clinician. That man was Fromm. I find it very interesting that Freud is talked about in every high school and explored more in college psychology programs, with little or no mention of his 'arch nemesis' Dr. Fromm.

   i. In Fromm's book he talks about how he thinks Freud got it all wrong. He roughly talks about Freud's perspective that our main drives in life are to satiate the animalistic qualities, i.e., sexual drive, and selfish desires. Freud's theory about how we are socially appropriate to get what we want. Fromm is the opposite. Fromm believed that the desires of a human are to be creative, pursue dreams/wishes, to give and get love. Fromm argues that our ability to talk and think critically was developed to create things to make our lives easier and we get joy out of testing our abilities.

   ii. If we were to talk about healing from trauma we would lean more towards Fromms' perspective. Freud would keep us stuck in this topic, while Fromm puts us on the right track. When a situation feels heavy or intense it is best to focus on creativity and developing ways to see yourself through the situation. When I work with people suffering from trauma we work on creativity. The more artistic and creative the more your brain can heal. This might include pushing yourself into a creative space. Learning how to dance, try to write a poem, pick up painting (yes, I guess you can sip and paint, but not always).

CHAPTER 5

Let's figure out what gets in your way?

1.) Let's be honest... it's probably you. I'm sure you're thinking, wow, talk about tough love. Some statements are best delivered clearly. Most people get in their own way. Here are some of the ways that it occurs.

    a. Self full-filling prophecy. The heck of it is that I'm not a prophet. I can't see the future. The sociological argument is that you can in fact guide events to become reality. The definition of a self-fulfilling prophecy has nothing to do with mind reading or fortune telling. The idea behind a self-fulfilling prophecy is that first you decide that something is true, then you mold everything you see to fit into that perspective or schema. Each little bit of information adds to turn events into occurring just as you have predicted. -Have you ever played the game, "Slug Bug?" This game works very much in this manner. The goal is to find a Volkswagen beetle vehicle, as soon as you see one you have to be the first to shout "Slug Bug" and then you get to punch the other passenger in the arm. People that play this game tend to see VW bugs everywhere. It's not exactly the same as a self-fulfilling prophecy, but the concept is that if you continue to look for something, you will quickly find it. If you are looking for something bad, you will find it. If you are looking for good, then you will also find it.

        i. Here's an example. Let's pretend that you are working at your dream job. You get hired and shortly after you begin to worry about losing the job. As each day progresses you find that you're spending more and more of your time and energy feeling anxiety about losing the job. This causes you so much stress that you find yourself becoming distracted at work. You interpret everything your manager says as accusatory and negative. The fear keeps you up at night. Soon, you are getting written up for poor performance. You convince yourself that your coworker is out to get you. Each interaction is interpreted with a negative lens. Within a few months you are let go. "You knew it, it was too good to be true."

ii. Keep in mind that the negative view and perspective walked you into a reality that was very uncomfortable. You didn't want to lose your job, but that's exactly what ended up happening, and quickly.

iii. Most people use self-fulfilling prophecies in a negative manner. However, I will let you in on a little secret, it can be used for good also. (Oh yes Obi Wan Kenobi) One can envision a positive outcome and work towards that reality. (How do you think I got through graduate school, not on good looks alone.)

b. The next area that may get in your way is the concept of secondary labeling. This is typically used as a social construct. Primary labeling is when someone outside of yourself labels you. For example, this would be if someone calls you a name. This name may be based on little to no information. A common example is let's say that the first time that you try smoking marijuana another peer see's you and calls you a 'burnout.' (For those of you un-hip to the lingo, a burnout is someone who spends all their time smoking pot and they are always burning the blunt. I don't know if with vaping it would still apply, but it might be a classic in name calling.) Anyway, in your mind you may rationalize that you can't be a 'burnout' this was only your first time. But the statement might slowly eat away at you. You may notice that soon you decide to smoke more frequently because it doesn't really matter if you're 'just a burnout anyway.' The key piece of secondary labeling is when you agree to the label that someone else placed upon you.

  i.   Secondary labeling can be very detrimental to one's ego. It makes quick work to erode one's confidence. A more frequent example may rest in a flippant statement from a parent. Let's say you make a mistake and your parent says, "Don't be so stupid." In fear of rejection, you may interpret that as, "You're so stupid." As time progresses you may find yourself making a mistake (while alone, maybe you trip or fall, a common and simple accident) but you say to yourself, "Why are you so stupid?" Or, "You're such an idiot" "What are you thinking? Are you even thinking?" There are many equal versions of this negative self-dialogue.

c. Guilt – As my uncle says, "FISH ON!" This means that you reel as fast and as hard as you can until you get that huge salmon on the boat. Well... if we are talking about guilt those are usually just as big and just as difficult to reel in. Look at the kinds of 'fish/guilt' we have = self-induced – manipulative - survivors– religious/devotional Ohh guilt. This is one of my favorites. Isn't it just wonderful? Guilt, for many people it is their main driving force in their world. It is what moves them through the day, feeling bad. I like guilt because it is so misunderstood and commonly inaccurately applied. While working with others I have (on many occasions) stopped someone from 'beating themselves up' and asked them this simple question,

  i.   "What, do you think, is the biological purpose of guilt?" In most cases I will earn a confused look as if they walked into an unseen wall.

  ii. My next question is, "Think of cavemen and now conceptualize why would they feel the emotion of guilt? How is this helpful?" This usually yields the response, "Nothing, it's not helpful," or "I've never thought of it as having a purpose or use." This response for me is exciting, it means that I'm successfully challenging your thinking and teaching you how to query those frustrating life experiences.

The basic response to this question is as follows. There are many types of guilt (which we will cover shortly) but there are two main ingredients in order to make guilt. These two items are 1) social interactions plus 2) regret of personal behavior. This regret is usually based on information that occurs after the 'injury' or behavior is completed. The main purpose of guilt is to understand how our behavior has affected another person. Upon reflection we may choose to dislike our behavior and 'regret' our choices. This will afford us the opportunity to change our actions in the future so that we do not negatively affect others. Remember, if you do not regret your behavior then one should not feel guilt.

It is important to remember that guilt is a social emotion. Humans are social creatures. Survival to the caveman depended on the teamwork approach. If you upset a leader, or a group of people, it could mean exile, which equaled certain death. Guilt has been a self-protection technique. We must be accepted by the group and be aware of how our behavior impacts others. In the day and age of isolation, Amazon, and delivery of food, we really do not need this protection mechanism as we once did, so remember, do I value the person that I'm 'feeling guilty' towards?

I caution people from guilt baths. This is where you just soak forever in this feeling of failure and badness. If you regret a behavior, then you need to make new behaviors or seek a way to remedy the error.

What are the types of guilt you ask? Why yes, I would love to elaborate! There are basically four types of guilt: basic-guilt, manipulative-guilt, survivors-guilt, and devotional guilt. I'm sure we could break these sections down further, but for now we will stick with these four.

1. Basic-guilt – this is traditional social guilt. These guilt items are more tied in with social grooming and appropriate behavior towards one another. While most people

believe that taking candy from a baby is the easiest thing one can do, it is also socially frowned upon. This involves behaving in a way that after introspection or feedback from others helps increase our awareness of how others perceive us. If we disagree with another's perspective, we are likely to take inventory and decide to modify our actions.

    a.   An example is if you find out a friend is sick and in the hospital. You mean to see them or send them flowers, but you forget. After you hear that they are out of the hospital. Another friend tells you that your entire cohort went and visited your ill friend. You discover that you are the only one that didn't reach out. With this information you feel bad that you didn't reach out to them. Optimally, the next time a friend is in the hospital you will reach out to them.

    b.   It should be noted that this is the healthiest version of guilt. It is used to be reflective and modify behavior to decrease negative emotions moving forward.

2.) Manipulative guilt is sadly the most common type of guilt. This is usually applied by those we are closest to. It can be family members or friends. There are two categories of manipulative guilt. One is secondary-gain guilt, and the other is mother's guilt. Secondary-gain guilt is based on the idea of trying to get others to feel an emotion and change your behavior to accommodate another person (often at the sacrifice of your happiness).

    a.   Secondary Gain Guilt : Yesterday I watched my younger daughter whine and complain because she wanted a specific item and the older daughter obliged and gave her the better object. I'm sure if we asked the oldest she would say that it was a sacrifice and that she felt manipulated to give it to her younger sister.

....

      b. This type of guilt is only successful if one of the parties believes that the world is fair and equal or if one of the parties is a 'people pleaser' or what I quickly call a 'giver.' The older daughter only gave over the toy because she believes that the younger will reciprocate, or she wants to please the younger sibling or even gain approval from parents. This is probably very common in the work-place when there is belief that others are watching or will take notice of these small gestures.

3.) Survivors' guilt is attached to grief. There are many books on grief and numerous ways to address these heavy and intense emotions. When one feels the loss of a loved one there is usually a moment where the survivor will feel intense 'guilt.' These emotions are often overwhelming and are more synonymous with a tornado, too many emotions swirling around to really pick out one item from another. Survivors' guilt can range from wishing they were deceased to not endure the pain of life without the loved one all the way to blaming themselves for not 'foreseeing' the future and changing it when they 'think' they could have in the past.

      a. This guilt gone unchecked by a professional can cascade into very destructive behavior and thoughts. This type of guilt rests more in the concept that we can control the future and possibly change it if we just would have 'read the signs' early enough. This is a very slippery slope into delusional thoughts that allow ourselves to be the 'bad guy/gal.' It can be much easier to beat ourselves up than allow anyone or anything else to 'make' us feel bad. I heed caution in becoming your own executioner.

            i. The irony of this concept that we can 'make' anyone feel is completely inaccurate. If it was true that we could 'make' others feel anything, then I would just tell someone to feel different and be out of a job. Also, if we had the power to 'make' anyone think

....

or feel a way then we would just 'make' all of mankind obey rules and never hurt anyone's feelings, because others would just 'make you' behave.

4.) Devotional guilt is the last type of guilt we will discuss. There are two types of devotional guilt. One is mothers' guilt where the intent is pure and to help you become more socially accepted while holding tightly to a sense of morality and ethics. "Treat others how you want to be treated" and so forth.

    a. Mother's Guilt: This one best embodies the main purpose of guilt. In this sub-type a parent, teacher, adult, or role model makes statements to yield embarrassment to the receiver (often the child during its developing stages) to make them respond differently. An example is when mom's apply pressure to get the children to respond in a socially pleasing manner. For example saying 'thank you' or 'please' while interacting with others. As an adult this is quite common with significant others and close friends.

    b. Religious Guilt is the next sub-type. Religious guilt is when a religious organization develops a structure of 'ethics or rules' that must be followed. If these are not followed then the individual is somehow either inherently 'bad' or must repent their misdeeds. There is a wide range of how intense this guilt can manifest itself. It can range from a small and tiny internal 'nagging voice' if you did not 'do the right thing.' It can also be as intense as a religious imposed punishment or self-imposed punishments. People in the medieval time frame (1530's) would flog themselves to punish and correct their 'evil' or 'mishaps.' In other words this aided in bringing salvation and driving out evil. These layers of 'wrong-doing' can range from punishment for 'thoughts' all the way up to 'actions.' The function of this guilt is similar to the mother's guilt (to build and guide you) and is applied more to adults staying on an ethical course.

i. It should be noted. When I see this form of guilt 'gone awry' it is usually when the individual reports feelings of 'guilt' for every imaginable thought or act and oftentimes events that are outside of their control (the acts of others or even unseen outcomes). Not only do the individuals experience chronic discomfort in the guise of guilt, but this also creates a new identity for their "God" where it is an entity that only exists to point out failings, faults, and errors. Every behavior has the opportunity to be twisted into a misdeed or 'evidence' of the individual person's shortcomings. This is often where religion and critical interpretation should have taken a left at Albuquerque.

CHAPTER 6

How do I screw my head on right?

This is a great question; I think everyone asks this during their life and those that don't ever ask it are clearly narcissistic or a socio-path. Us in the biz would call that a 'rule-out question.' It helps narrow down the possibilities or type of disorder. There is little to be done with those that have not asked that question or something similar, but for the rest of us that get lost in our behavior or question ourselves, here are a few ways to push forward. There is a fun song in country music genre that says, "What was I thinking?" In the song he describes a series of poor thought out behaviors mostly for the attention of a pretty woman. I think that most of us have made decisions in our life that in the moment seemed okay, good, or not problematic, but as time went on, we found ourselves reflecting and wondering why we said or did what we had.

1.) Let us focus on self-care to get these wheels spinning.

    a. My favorite concept is the 'Airplane Technique'. It is simple and to the point. This is also my favorite for those that really enjoy guilt, people pleasing, and caregivers (who are notoriously known for horrid self-care).

    b. Those that have been on a plane (and those that haven't I will walk you through). Once everyone is seated in their assigned seat and all your luggage is stored or whisked to the bottom of the plane because it's overbooked, the flight attendants will go through the exact same safety procedure regardless of the airline. It will start with the complexity of fastening your seat belt, then remind you that the super comfortable seat under your 'derriere' doubles as a floatation device. (Personally, I pray that the floatation portion is more effective than the comfort of the cushion portion.) They remind you to look for the nearest exit row and lastly, here is your pop quiz....

i.   They remind you that if the cabin pressure should change an oxygen mask will drop down from the ceiling and you should....

    a.   First - put the mask on the child next to you

    b.   First - Put the mask on yourself

    c.   Grab as many masks as possible so you will improve your chances of survival over your fellow passengers.

    d.   Push the call button for assistance while screaming in terror.

ii.   In the 20+ years I have asked this question, people have only chosen a. or b. Interestingly enough most of my caregivers or those that shower in a hefty dose of daily guilt will say (a). Their rationale is that they must take care of others or the person next to them.

iii.   In reality the answer is (b). You have to put the mask on yourself first and then you can help your neighbor. If you pass out while you are assisting the child next to you, then you have just created two patients instead of one temporarily.

iv.   The bottom line is that you can't help anyone if you can't help yourself. You wouldn't hire an out of shape personal trainer because you need to believe in someone that believes in themselves first.

v.   Remember, self-care is NOT selfish, but essential for those that want to help others.

vi.   Lastly, you teach others how you want to be treated. If you are always putting yourself last then soon those around you will start to agree. Soon, you will be helped last if you are helped at all.

2.) Best practices for bad behaviors

    a.   Bad behaviors cannot be avoided. This isn't to say that we just give into our visceral impulses, but this is to increase our understanding that part of the learning process in life is to make mistakes. When we make such mistakes it's important to keep in mind a few 're-directions.'

         i.   There are two main options, one is to make that bad decision with an open and honest framework. Be honest with yourself. I'm going to make this choice X and it will likely have one of these two outcomes.

        ii.   When working with addiction, of any kind, it's important to know our history and the likelihood of future outcomes. When someone with alcoholism says, "I'm not like those other alcoholics, I can have A drink." I encourage the person to explain to me the frequency of that history. Can they have 'One' drink? Or do they start with one and that leads to the impulse for multiple. When I have these individuals be honest with themselves, I say, "You can have that 'first' drink only if you're honest with yourself at the beginning and you are willing to undertake those consequences. So, you must say to yourself, "I'm going to start drinking and I will likely wake up in jail, the hospital, or end up at the morgue." Or whatever their typical drinking pattern looks like, maybe it's calling up ex's and yelling at them, or risky sexual behavior, or gambling. Then and only then, can you take that first sip. It is imperative that we are honest with ourselves and not downplay our actions and behaviors. It is when we downplay the outcome that we are lying to ourselves and later tend to feel overwhelmed with feelings of guilt and self-damnation.

    b.   Once a bad behavior or choice is made it is important to 'mitigate damage'. The old phrase, "In for a penny in for a pound" is shit advice. This phrase is very permissive of bad behavior and it's not true. If you are in for a penny, then you are only in for a penny, you are the one that decides if you're going to invest more time, energy, or money into the situation. (That phrase started as a British phrase, a pound was a form of currency greater than a penny, the best example would be a dollar. So think of it as in for a penny in for a dollar.)

i. The best way to minimize damage is to stop making more damage and assess the situation. I call this option the 'Car Accident Approach.' I call it this because I have a nice visual to help you reframe on your own. If you get into an accident with your car and hit another vehicle, what typically happens? We stop our car, get out of the vehicle (if we are physically able to) and check on the safety of the other car's driver. After that we look at the damage to our vehicle (We get super pissed-off). Then we call the police or first responders and continue from there.

ii. What we don't do is get into an accident and then if the vehicle is drivable or not too damaged, reverse the vehicle and slam it into the other car again and again until the car is totaled. We don't continue this bad behavior. We don't continue to crash into the other vehicle until there is too much irreparable damage. If we don't take this approach with a car accident, why would we take this approach with other goals that we missed.

iii. If you're on a diet and eat a piece of cake at a party, it makes no sense to stop and get a fast-food meal and ice cream on your way home because you "messed up anyway." Instead, stop after the cake and consider if you are upset with your behavior and ascertain another way to approach those situations moving forward. Think of this mathematically. If you unintentionally added 375 calories (with the cake), then you are plus 375 calories. If you add fast food 1250 calories and ice cream 650 calories (1900) and now the cake from earlier you are 2275 ahead from your original objective. In for a penny in for a pound does not make sense. In this example you are in for a 'lot' of pounds (not the British money).

       iv.   Remember, after a bad choice/statement/follow through it's important to stop making decisions and assess the next goal. So... in a sense, after we hit another car, get out of the vehicle, and assess the damage.

3.) Levels of Development – where are you?... Why is this important? Why, thank you for asking. There are multiple theories of human development. The one that I find the most helpful while working with others is this three-layered version. Understanding this concept will help you understand others that upset or frustrate you regularly. Many times, if you can comprehend the other person's perspective then you can find ways to get along better. If you can understand the perspective in which they view the world then you can find a way to get common ground.

    a.   The first layer is *dependency*. Every person experiences this phase of development. Now, some people never move out of this level. As a child in this phase, you are 'dependent' upon your teachers, parents, and other adults in your life to teach and provide those basic do's and don'ts. Some adults never transition out of the dependency phase. An adult that is in the 'dependency' level is someone who never moved forward, they became stuck. These people become adults that are not accountable for their own behavior. They depend on others. It may be the government, or parents, or friends, etc. who provide all their financial needs and people in this phase also hold those others responsible if they are not happy or satisfied. People in the dependent phase will blame others for periods of dissatisfaction, "It would have worked out if 'YOU' wouldn't have _____" There are many examples. Financially they are parasitic in nature and only chose selfish paths to get their own needs met. They tend to view failures as the result of someone else not doing what they 'should have'. There is minimal to no 'self-reflection.'

    b.   The next level is *independent*. During this phase you realize that you can make your own money and feel a sense of accomplishment. There becomes an understanding that you don't need anyone, and you can be self-sufficient. Once there is a successful transition then some people in this phase tend to hold resentment or disdain for those that are still in the dependent phase of development. The people that are in 'independence' take great pride in their accomplishments and the fact that they don't 'need' anyone to survive or make it in the world. If you are in this group, you realize that you can make your own money, and essentially survive without the help of anyone else.

The challenge in this group is that you become so satisfied in your 'independence' that you will often snub those you love or care about. The problem develops when you tell others that "I can do it myself, I don't need you." At that point it is a matter of time before others in your life start to believe you and 'leave.' People need to be needed and if you create an environment where people don't feel needed then they will leave. They will go where they are needed.

c. The last phase is *interdependency.* During this phase you have shifted out of independence by viewing yourself and others as more of a community. During this level you place more value in others than just one-self. It becomes more valuable to include others and integrate well with others. You have a strong understanding of your own strengths and weaknesses and lean on others to help you. You ask others to help you not because you 'deserve' it or 'need' it, but because you want them to feel appreciated and it's not your strong trait. Very few people make it to this position. It is hard to be this self-aware and interactive.

4.) Another place that you can get stuck is in your own thoughts. There is a great theoretical orientation called Access Consciousness. (There are classes available to get full training if you are interested.) One of the objectives with this orientation is to better assess your thoughts. One of the tasks that can be assigned is to write down every thought that you think in a 24-hour period. This is a very daunting task and takes a while. After you write down every thought you look at the general theme. Then after you look for a theme you write down 'who does this thought originate with?' Once you examine your 'thoughts' and inner voice you will see that most phrases come from someone else. (The argument in this theory is that no thought originates with you, that all thoughts come from someone else.) The next thing you do is ask yourself, "Do I agree with this statement?" It will be at that time that you can better determine if you want to keep some of this internal dialogue.

    a.   Let's practice.

        i.   Imagine that some of your self-talk is... "I'm so stupid, they probably think that I'm a fool, there I go embarrassing myself again."

        ii.   If we break this up then we can see that the self-talk is very critical and negative. They also highlight that others think poorly of this person.

            1.   Who first said 'you're stupid?' Maybe it was a sibling, a neighbor, etc.

            2.   Who said, "You're a fool?"

            3.   Who described you as an embarrassment?

        iii.   The further you dissect these intimate thoughts the more you discover that these are not your own sentiments, but rather those of family, friends, teachers, or co-workers. And when you get down to it, what do they know anyway? Be adamant that who you are is more than the sum of other people's opinions, especially if these are opinions that, after inspection, you 'wouldn't buy their book!'

5.) Oh GREAT (said in a moody adolescent voice) another story.

    Here comes the GREAT story, well... what makes it so great? Excellent question, just sit back and listen. The moral of the story is that *what we focus on becomes what we see.* If we want to funnel negative or positive energy, we receive a rebound of the same energy in return. That wonderful phrase, "You reap what you sow" comes to mind. But if you are not a farmer or don't think you look good in overalls, then this story might be more relatable.

Many years ago, I was overcoming an intense knee and hip injury. After about six months of rehab, I was ready to attempt running again. I had a race and I needed to get my body prepared. I enlisted one of my very fit and athletic friends Tony. We showed up to a high school track and Tony said, "How are you feeling?" I said, "Well, I've got on a pretty flexible knee brace and my medications are mostly working." We started training with a light trot. Tony said, "How ya doing?" I responded by informing him of all the areas that had pain. I explained the radiating throbs up my hip. I shared how out of breath I was and lamented how out of shape I was in general. I was able to share every discomfort I was experiencing for our 30-minute practice.

The next time we met up and Tony asked, "How are you feeling today?" I responded like I did the first time, sharing how I was in pain and the limited range of motion my knee was experiencing. We started jogging and every time he asked how I was doing I made sure to explain every ailment in detail.

The third time we met up Tony asked me how I was doing. I said, "Well..." and before I was able to elaborate on my discomfort, he cut me off and Tony said, "The answer from this point on is 'GREAT'. In fact, I want you to smile and give me a thumbs up AND if I don't believe what you are saying I will ask again until I believe you. I need a thumbs up and GREAT every time." I was surprised, but since he was the expert, I complied.

The first time Tony asked me I said "great?" He looked at me and said, "What did you say?" in that official voice. I responded, "Great" and added a thumbs up. He then said, "I don't think I heard you?" So, I responded in my best, "I'M GREAT!" I smiled and gave two thumbs up. As the running went on, he continued to ask, and I sold my overzealous excitement. This went on for many weeks. As time went on, I did start to feel better and stronger.

When it came time for me to run, I actually performed great. I laughed while I was running at how 'great' it felt to get my body back when there was a time that I couldn't see a full recovery. I was able to finish that race without walking for the first time in years. When you are pushing through a tough time, there are moments that if you focus on the discomfort then you will only see the bad or difficult. If you can harness the desired energy or even focus on the outcome or the goal, you my friend, may find yourself performing "GREAT!"

CHAPTER 7

It's not me... It's you

There are moments in our lives where after we have certain interactions, we come to the enlightenment of... "you're the one that's not making sense."

What's interesting is that usually during the beginning of therapy, individuals are very scared or concerned that they will be told that they are 'Crazy' or that they will snap and 'become crazy.' I usually take the time to remind those people that first of all we (mental health professionals) don't use the term crazy, that is a colloquial word. In mental health it is usually described as someone with 'reality testing concerns/limitations.' What is important to remember is sane people fear becoming 'insane.' Insane people believe that 'you are insane.' People that have reality testing issues are unable to view any problems or concerns with their behavior (there is no insight).

Here comes where the rubber meets the sand dune. What? Yes, when we deal with people, they are too variable and frequently we can't get the traction that we so desperately desire. In an attempt to teach people the difference in others I have created an over-simplified model. The purpose of this is to clearly divide people up into two groups to better determine if it is 'Me' or 'You.'

1.) These two options are Slot machines / vending machines. People will fit into one of two groups. They are either a slot machine or a vending machine.

a. Slot machines are sexy, loud, attention grabbers, fun, adventurous, seductive, bright and initially so much fun. (Keep in mind the emphasis on 'initially' fun).

    i. Let's explore slot machines (the physical machine) for a bit. They ping at humans most frequent behavioral response, Random Reinforcement. Humans are drawn into this concept of random reinforcement. This type of reinforcement is where people are sucked into gambling, addictions (to include video games and even the dreaded facebook/social media), abusive relationships, etc.

        1.) People that are slot machines need to take. In order to take, someone must give. A problem will emerge if the 'giver' ever wants something in return. 'Takers' don't give easily.

        2.) Now, imagine that you are at a casino, you see this great slot machine and it says, "Yes, you, come here, I'll give you a huge payoff for just a nickel." Who could say no to that? Anyway, humans will be drawn to this advertisement and sit in front of the machine. They will put their nickel in and pull the lever (for those that have been in a casino lately you are aware that my image is outdated, but far more nostalgic). When you place the first nickel into the slot let's say the machine is programmed for a 1 in 20,000 payout. Now, I want you to figure out the math, what is the payout amount for the 5th consecutive nickel you put into the machine?

           a. Is it 5 in 20,000

           b. Or 1 in 20,000

        3.) If you guessed the second option then you would be correct (depressed, but correct).

        4.) The challenge is that our human logic is driven from years of conditioning. That training has said, if you work hard, or practice for a long time that it will pay off. While those concepts are accurate with learning an instrument or improving in athletics, it is not accurate with all people. Remember when you work hard on reading or a talent you are the variable, as soon as you add people, all bets are off.

   a. We tend to think, "If I just love them more, or show love more. If I just change the way I react. If I.... I....I....I" Well, you are not a pirate, so ey ey ey will not make a difference.

   b. We will put more energy into a person that seems fun and charming because we want more of that excitement. We are drawn to chaos the same way we can't look away from a car accident.

ii. For the joy of it, let's return to the vending machine. While this beauty is a bit bland and far less flashy, it is sturdy and reliable. It is dependable and consistent.

   1. The best part about a vending machine is it offers you something FOR something. In most cases it offers food or drink for a monetary amount. If you put a dollar into the machine you do not get a dollar back, BUT even better, you get something that you value to be worth a dollar. Hence there is more of a give and take or a push and pull dynamic.

      a. This is a far more balanced concept.

      b. While it may be crude on its initial glance it may be more beneficial to start dividing others into one of two categories until you can learn to understand any underlying themes or drives. Remember... Save the slot machines for the casinos, not your personal life, yikes, nobody wants snake eyes!!!

Illustration by Richard Heger

b. Weeds/Parasites

i. "Mom, when I grow up I want to be a weed or a parasite, I want to find ways to take what others have worked hard for and make them feel like shit for keeping it, muahhahaha. I think I'll become a parasite on those I care about." Said by a child. In response mother says, "Oh dear, well make sure it's not me or your father and we'll support that selfish decision."

1. While I've worked with some people with very poor judgment, I don't think anyone would actually say these things out loud or encourage their children to actively choose this lifestyle. Let's explore the life of a weed or parasite a bit further.

c. While living in Belize for an undergraduate class I discovered some of the most fascinating intricate models of weeds or parasites. There was an entire study group dedicated to learning the workings of the mahogany tree. (Interesting fact, the tree has to be over 500 years old before it can be harvested) The tree is absolutely amazing and beautiful in life and is very rare. They do not grow near one another and are fickle in their reproduction (similar to panda's) and do not like to be 'artificially' grown. The mahogany tree is so large that it has enormous 'buttresses' . These are like ropes on a tent pulled tight to keep the tree up because it is so heavy and tall. I have a picture of our study group in front of one. It was about 20 feet tall. There were four of them to support the tree.

i.   I want you to think of someone that is strong with a personality that is larger than life. Those people tend to have their own support network or as I call it, their 'entourage' (which must be said with a rich British accent). The stronger the buttress, the taller and stronger it will become. We need a strong support network.

ii.   As we explore these parasites we will see that the goal of the weed is to live off the mahogany until it can grow enough to strangle out a branch and eventually the entire tree. It will grow beyond the rainforest canopy to steal the sun from the tree.

Photo from Fort Leavenworth (see parasites grow everywhere, not just Belize).

d. There were two main kinds that we studied. One of the weeds would be long and thin and grow from the rainforest ground up until it caught a branch and then start to suffocate the branch. Another one would be a seed that would float until it landed on a branch and grow down to the rainforest floor and start to wrap itself around the base. If the buttresses were well developed it was much harder for this version to get a good hold onto the tree.

    a. I want to point out that when people 'do well' or 'make-it' there tends to be a buttress of people that remain helpful and supportive while a few 'parasites' or 'fair-weather friends' appear to ride the wave of success.

    b. Studies of lottery winners have proven this phenomenon. Several people that have won the lottery report feeling heightened levels of depression due to the influx of people that they barely knew, or relatives that have been absent that appear and continue to hound the person and ask for 'help'. These people are parasitic in nature, and it can be hard to really separate these two things, especially if this is someone that you have wanted to develop a healthy relationship towards.

Photo from Fort Leavenworth, see how the second tree is asphyxiating the primary tree in the middle.

2.) Rules of Compliments/criticisms

    a.   This is one of my favorites! This rule is there to keep you safe, not only from others, but more importantly, from yourself! We all fall prey to allowing others words or statements to cause long term damage. We often allow these words to become squatters in our heads. Remember that not all compliments or criticisms are correct/true/or valuable. We want our food to have expiration dates and go through a screening process. We need the words from others to also go through a screening process.

    b.   There are three rules that must be followed. They are the same rules whether it is a compliment or a criticism. Here we go....

Number 1

Is the compliment/criticism plausible? *(Meaning, is there any way in any framework that the statement could be correct.)*

* If 'NO' then you must reject (no need to move onto next question)

* If "YES' then you go onto the next question

Number 2

Is the author (person who said it) a 'subject matter expert'? (Meaning, is this person a fashion editor or an expert in the topic they are providing their opinion?)

*If 'NO' then you must reject (no need to move onto the next question)

*If 'YES' then you go onto the next question

Number 3

Last, is the statement for secondary gain? (Basically, is this for manipulation, a way to get you to bend to their will or have them get their way?)

*If 'YES' then you must reject.

*If 'NO' then you would accept.

You just need one of these three to not fit and the whole thing must be rejected. Now, that is not to say that you couldn't gain some extra knowledge from feedback from others. But I caution you on how you choose to integrate that information.

Let's re-examine this through a compliment and criticism standpoint.

1.) Let's say that your coworker says, "You only got the special assignment because you're the boss's pet."

    a. 1) Plausible, - Is it plausible that you only got the assignment because you are the boss's pet = Possibly

    b. 2) Reliable source – The co-worker has been at the place for many years = Yes/possibly

    c. 3) Secondary Gain – The co-worker has a history of bullying people out of special projects in the past. This was only said to get you to feel bad and maybe step down as lead on the project. = Yes (this was said for secondary gain/manipulation).

    d. Our answers are 1) possible 2) Yes/possible 3) Yes – We must reject. It was not said to be helpful, it was said to manipulate. We have to deny this criticism. Remember a true criticism is meant to help us improve a weakness.

2.) On the flip side, let us imagine that you have some self-esteem challenges. Like sometimes you wake up and your emotions rolled off the bed and are on the floor. Well... it's time to mop them up, wring them out into a glass and if it's half full then drink up!! If not... well... don't be greedy and just take what you can get.

    a. Where was I going with that... oh yes, I remember, for those of you that are shitty at accepting compliments, *you know who you are*, you unintentionally shit on everyone who is nice to you because your self-esteem never got mopped up and is still strewn all over the floor. Well, just pick that up and follow these three rules.

        i. 1.) Is the compliment plausible?

  ii. 2.) Is it from a reliable source?

  iii. 3.) Is it for secondary gain/manipulation?

b. One of the mental health facilities I worked at we spent one day of training learning to give and receive compliments. Yes, that sounds bizarre, I thought the same thing. As the class went on it was so obvious that for most people they are 'out of their element' with positive statements. The most common error is the 'rejection' statement. For example: "Ooh, that's such a pretty dress!" Response: "What, this old thing, I'm surprised it still fits."

  i. While you may feel negative about yourself or embarrassed you just (hopefully unintentionally) told the person that you think their ideas are bad or wrong. They said something nice and you responded in a cutting way. Even though in your mind you may think that as long as the negative is about yourself that it's acceptable. The truth is that if you wouldn't say those cutting things about a dear friend, then you can't say them about yourself. Let's roll through an example of accepting a compliment.

  ii. Let's say a coworker says, "You're really fast with those TPS reports." If you disagree with them, you say, "Thank you." If you agree with them you say, "Thanks it took me a few months, but with the help of the Bob's I have it down." For practice, let's use the rules with this example.

   1.) Is it plausible? Yes, I could be fast with the TPS reports

   2.) Is it from a reliable source? Possibly, this coworker must complete the same task.

3.) Is it for secondary gain? Maybe, they might want my help or guidance, but it's not malevolent in nature.

4.) In conclusion, I must accept the compliment! Even if accepting the compliment means my low self-esteem might be forced into middle self-esteem.

3.) One of my preferred reframes on compliments and criticism is in a simple question. When we hear negative feedback, we tend to accept it at full value, while compliments are quickly minimized and ignored. In order to pull that 'middle self-esteem' to 'high self-esteem' we can use this reframe.

   a. When you hear a compliment or criticism go through the three questions, after that you can try this approach and ask yourself this question, "Would I go to this person for advice?" If the answer is yes, then accept the statement. If the answer is 'no' then you must reject that statement.

   b. Humans tend to accept negative/bad more readily than we agree with the positive. This is a dynamic that needs to shift, especially internally. So put on that weight belt and let's do a deadlift with that self-esteem. "One, two heave ho."

4.) One of the biggest challenges I see with couples or long standing friends involves the misconception of time. One of the very common pitfalls that occurs is when we (all of us do this!) believe that if we've known someone for long enough that we continue to live in the memories of the beginning of that relationship and never see them as the person in front of us today. This can be a positive or a negative perception.

   a. For those that 'wrong' us or hurt our feelings or lie or make a mistake we may not ever let them survive the gauntlet of obstacles to keep them shackled in those past errors. Their prison sentence will never end and without chances for rehabilitation, we refuse to see growth and enjoy our grudge. In order to be rooted in the negative past one must stay and remind the other by standing on those proverbial village steps while ringing the bell of previous injustice "Dong, Dong, Dong"

b.   Those on the opposite spectrum, suffer equally, but on the opposing end. Those that continue to see the positive in the person, despite the clear absence of current events also remain trapped. (When I say absence, I mean that there is a significant drop. It means that they are cruel or hurtful more often than they are helpful and nurturing. The scales have shifted.) The problem is that this sentence is self-imposed and is derived from desperately wanting to see positive behaviors in someone who has not displayed them for a significant period of time.

When I worked in the prisons we would call this *toxic hopefulness*. This means that one person remains so hopeful that they stop seeing the reality and long for a return to the past. This is the pattern in domestic abuse. Remember domestic abuse can be physical, sexual, verbal/emotional, and neglect. Many people stay in these situations with the hope that the person they fell in love with at the beginning will make a return visit. They hope that one day the other person will wake up and see their value. Businesses call this the sunk cost fallacy. This is the phenomenon where people continue an endeavor once time/energy/money has been invested. People will continue to invest because they want it to work out despite the current information. People will continue to invest even when it's better to cut their losses.

One time I saw a man at a casino. He was clearly inebriated and he was at the roulette table. His friends were trying to get him to walk away and he kept betting more saying, "I need to win my $500 back. I have to keep putting in until I win it back." Shortly, after that the pit boss went over there and offered him a free steak for his $500 investment into the casino. This man was stuck in the sunk cost fallacy. While he should have cut his losses and left, he was determined to 'win it all back.' It is important to remember that casinos have all the staff and flashy lights because you 'aren't supposed to win all the time (if ever).'

c. So... what is a *significant* period of time? A basic rule to follow is in a short and then long 'recent' reflection. The short reflection lies in the last six months. The long reflection is in the past two years. It's safe to say that we all change and we are not stagnant. Some people change more rapidly than others. This is why we need to review people and their behavior (not words) more frequently. If you run a business you won't look at the sales from 10 years ago. You should look at the current trends. It's safe to apply similar expectations to those around you.

d. Remember that this 'assessment' would be best if you became reflective upon yourself.

    i. 'Are you behaving in a way or manner that is consistent with your perception of yourself?'

    ii. 'How could you make changes to ensure those goals?'

e. So... picture a montage, you know, like the one Rocky had. As psychologists our theme song (because it was repeated so frequently) was "Don't Rationalize with someone that is Irrational." The idea is that when illogic is the framework, there is no amount of logic that will dismount those thoughts. (It's like multiplying by zero, the answer is always zero). I guess we could even use the old Kenny Rogers song, "Know when to hold them, know when to fold them, know when to walk away, know when to run." These should be songs playing in the back of your mind as well, especially if you are interacting with someone who is 'not making sense.'

    i. One of my favorite stories is one in which my ego came into direct contact with irrationality or a delusion. The background for this is I was working in an inpatient long-term care facility. Most of the people there were being placed back on medication and undergoing psychological and pharmacological interventions in order to be returned to a life of independence with the help of a few services. When I began at the facility the previous psychologist explained that "Mary" was very high functioning and suffered from one delusion, "she believed she was pregnant." When I heard this, I thought, "well, that's easy, we'll get her on the road to recovery and get her out of here quickly." Two years later (yes, two years later) I decided to do the thing forbidden in psychology, I decided to test the integrity of her delusion. I thought, "You're so good at helping people (my inflated ego), Mary was a successful business woman and is so bright, let's just try to shake her of this delusion."

ii. I proceeded to do all the things a logical person would do. I offered to give her a pregnancy test. She declined, "Why would I take a test to prove something I already know is true?" It went on and on like this, without me gaining any traction. I asked, "Mary, we've been together for two years and the normal gestational period is nine months, how can you explain this." Her response was at first to laugh at me, (silly little psychologist), then she said, "That's why I'm here, I'm part of an experimental program to extend the length of pregnancy. The goal is to have a child that comes out more independent and self-sufficient." (On a side note, that would be pretty cool) I gave my rationalization a break until one day I came in to discover others were sharing in with her delusion. I had another client knitting baby shoes. As I inquired, she said, "Oh it's so wonderful, Mary had her baby." Well, you can imagine my excitement. If she had this baby, then it would mean that she is no longer pregnant. I raced to her room and asked, 'where is the baby?' She responded, "At the hospital of course." I then said, "So does this mean you are no longer pregnant?" She looked at the dim-witted psychologist and said, "As soon as I had the baby, they put a new embryo in, so I'm still pregnant." It was at that moment that all my hopes of logic were dashed. It was a hard lesson to learn, but if I would have only stayed with our montage music I would have prevented my blunder. So... remember kids... if someone is irrational, stop trying to make them see your point. Listen to Kenny Rogers and fold the cards and walk away from them, ever seeing it from your perspective.

5.) Don't let the bastards get you down – No Lite Illegitemos Contrere Vos

a. This next story is not mine, but belongs to someone dear to me. This story appeared at a time in my life when I was trying to make sense of someone being hurtful or unkind to me. I don't recall the events that lead up to the teaching point because the part that resonated was the moral of the story, so here it goes: Sometimes there are bad people, or the big bad wolf. It is not worth the time and energy to understand why they are a wolf, it is just important for you to identify that they are a wolf. The earlier you can identify, the safer you will be.

b. There are times that the wolf doesn't want to eat you, but merely wants to see you sweat and stress over making three different houses (straw/sticks/bricks). They want to see if they have the power to make you upset and struggle. Here is a Soldier's story about that experience.

c. This dear friend Joe was deployed overseas during the Vietnam war. He was on a special operations team who went places that he 'never really was.' On a rare opportunity a pilot who was doing reconnaissance asked him if he wanted to go on a mission and look out for enemy activity. In his eagerness for a change of pace he quickly agreed. Once they got into the air the pilot started making these very risky maneuvers. The worst part of these maneuvers was the effects on Joe's stomach. The pilot would drop the plane, then recover and ask Joe, "How ya feeling?" The plane was set up with the seats back-to-back so the pilot couldn't fully see Joe behind him. When the pilot asked, Joe would respond, "Great, with his thumbs up in the air and smiling as if he was having a great time. The pilot then

did barrel rolls with the plane and afterwards he would ask Joe, "How ya feeling?" Keep in mind that Joe's perception of the situation was that this guy was just trying to make him throw up and get the best of him. It now became Joe's mission to fight his impulse to puke. Joe would put his thumbs up and say, "Great." This went on for a few more times. Each question was met by a thumbs up and "Great." When Joe retells the story he says that with every "Great" he gives to the pilot the contents of his stomach are rising up higher and higher. The last "Great" had his lunch sitting at the base of his throat. On this last "Great" the pilot responded, "Well, you're no fun" and returned the plane back to headquarters. The moral of the story is "Don't let the bastards get you down." There will always be people who will push you to see if they can get a negative reaction out of you. Every time you react, you let them win a piece of yourself.

d. When people push you too far we often say, 'I just LOST control.' Call the police and send out an APB (all points bulletin) and get a search party together... I just 'lost control.' The police officer says, "Well Ma'am, what did your control look like before you lost it? What was it wearing? What picture would go on a milk carton?' As we can see, this sounds ridiculous. The truth about 'control' is that we choose to manage it or mismanage it.

    i. Even prison has bullies, but what is a bully? When the word is used we typically picture some bigger kid with a bad haircut pushing a smaller kid against the school wall and demanding money or food. When we move into adolescence it molds and expresses itself in the form of 'peer pressure.' As we become adults it can be transformed into 'guilt.' "Come on... please...why not... What's the big deal?" So on and so forth.

    ii. One of the prison's I worked at, the entire psychology team spent a great deal of time talking about 'emotional control.' The motivation for our discussions was activated after a physical altercation. Typically (depending on the prison) after someone is placed into segregation a psychologist will go and do an assessment for risk and safety. On a number of occasions, I would walk into the segregation area and go up to the window and ask the inmate, "So, what happened?" Ninety percent of the time I heard, "I lost control." That was followed by... <u>PERSON</u> kept pushing me and pissed me off so I **a)** screamed/ punched the person or **b)** took it out on the guard and screamed at him/her. My response was also the same, I would say, "No, you did not LOSE control, you HANDED over control. You allowed yourself to be managed by that other person." One of the greatest challenges in life is that we think that other people 'make us' or 'push us' to behave. In reality, no one (outside of physically putting hands on you) can MAKE you feel any way. We can let others manipulate us, or we can decide to be in charge of our emotions and feelings even in the opposition of those with very large and dynamic personalities. When others say something that upsets you, or feels like they are trying to upset you

1. Stop

2. Take a breath

3. Think, "Is this person worthy of my emotions, or should I hand over my reactions and become a puppet for this <u>PERSON</u>?"

iii. The objective is by the end of this exercise, you begin to feel like you alone start to 'own' your emotions without allowing others to push you in a direction that you would not have chosen on your own.

6.) Fromm vs Freud

a. I'm going to make a dramatic assumption here... you've heard of this guy called Sigmund Freud. Maybe it's from great Saturday night live skits, or the famous movie "What about Bob?" or you woke up from that sensational nap during high school intro to psychology class and heard his name waver in and out of consciousness. In any capacity, those of us in the 'biz' learn about him early on in graduate school. It is important to know that the man is either loved or hated in the community. Some people find his concepts dramatic and hyper focused on sex or animalistic tendencies. What most psychologists do agree on with reference to Freud is the many defense mechanisms that people develop. (Psst, this is the way you react to criticism or negative information) The other concept is the id, ego, and superego. These are basically the different parts of ourselves and how we approach situations to get our needs met. The next common agreement is about the phases of development, oral, anal, phallic, etc. The idea is that disorders are derived from a phase becoming stuck. Colleges tend to spend less time on the later years where they feel like he left his origins of neurological and psychological focus and started working out his own psychological challenges masked in the concept of theories and science.

    i.   If you allow me to oversimplify (which will make every psychodynamic psychologist clutch their pearls and point an accusatory finger in my direction) I would say that Freud saw humans through the lens of an animal with communication. They are all selfish and self-preserving and the brain is more closely tied to animalistic drives than any sense of altruism. Basically, if he had a top pop single on the charts it would be, "Me me me and I I I."

b. We've already introduced Fromm (the opposition) earlier in the book. Remember this man was Freud's counterpoint. He believed that humans developed cognition in order to dream, hope, create, and develop. He believed that if someone is loved or finds love that they will become more creative. He saw humans from a positive framework. More along the lines of humans seek out love and affirmation, not just selfish drives/desires. Spoiler alert, this guy didn't gain much traction in modern day psychology. In fact, he rarely ever gets an honorable mention in graduate school 'history of psychology' courses. Maybe because Freud did a great job of barring him or maybe people are secretly drawn to negative and only gave Freud the limelight. Or maybe we really are just animals, but in any case, there used to be a man that believed that our self-actualization and cognition were developed to create more good. Eric Fromm... We will miss you, good Sir. His top 40 hit would be, "All we need is love."

c. After working in psychology for over 20 years, I think that humans can be a conglomerate of both. Both sides provide great merit, but at the end of the day humans are far too complex to fit in a tidy box. It will be beneficial to see each person for their single contributions and their limitations. Limitations may include that concept of nature versus nurture. The root of that argument rests in the idea that we are a product of genetics or environment. We can argue all day on this concept. Debates may include that the environment will unlock certain genetics and genetics dictate the environmental factors. This debate has been demonstrated in many studies over the years. One common argument is about violence in video games. There is a belief that video games make children violent (Nurture) and the other statement is that violent children are drawn to video games (Nature). If we keep up these arguments then we will always come to the conclusion that nobody is actually watching the children. After we recover the children that are out and about doing stupid things unsupervised, we will need to have two separate rooms for the party and keep everyone in the 'proper space.'

d. Animalistic vs. Hope/Dreams. Freud was a fan of the id, ego, and superego. We can get into all that, but nah... The one cent version (three cents due to inflation) is that we are all lusty greedy animals that use creative social cues and skills to get our needs met. Our entire existence is barricading our animalistic desires up into a cave that gets one hour of recreation time a day (or something to that effect). The opposite perspective is that we have our cognition and creativity because we all desire to grow and be creative and make our lives better through inventions and dreams/passions.

....

    i.   At the end of the day I think they are both right and both wrong. I believe that humans are somewhere on that spectrum. Moving from selfish desires/needs to having hopes, dreams and being creative. Some people spend more time on one side of the pendulum than others.

  e. Fromm spent a great deal of time talking about LOVE, but also working on the ways that we can understand if with more psycho-babble, yeah, that way we sound super duper serious. If you ever get the urge to read his book (The Art of Love) I would recommend it, but keep in mind, it's a bit heavy. One of the best 'takeaways,' from the book is his concept of parental conditional vs unconditional love. This one is fun because I either get "ah-ha's" or I get, "I don't agree." Let's see what side you land on in this concept.

    i.   Fromm said that in a "healthy parental relationship." Now, I know, this is the place where I will lose most of you because now it sounds like fiction. I assure you that by the time we are done you will know that I'm not talking about make-believe, but rather a concept of healthy functioning. (Keep in mind that Fromm does dive into the unhealthy, so if you need a juxtaposition, it will be provided.) So... to finish, in a healthy parental relationship the Mother provides unconditional love and the Father provides conditional love.

      1.   Let's start with unconditional love. This one is supposed to be given by the mother. In this the mother provides you with all the love you could ever need at birth. There are pros and cons with this concept. The con is that at birth you are maxed out, which means you can never get any more. There is no action you can take to be more impressive or loved more deeply. The pro is that it can never be taken away from you. You can make bad choices and behaviors

....

and still fall freely into the open embrace of the mother.

2. Next is conditional love. This one is supposed to be provided by the father. The con to conditional love is that you can lose it. There can be a time/event that you are no longer the recipient of this awesome love stash. The pro is that you can always perform a behavior that will allow you to make more. You can gain more favor, compete with a sibling, etc. You can 'earn' the love back through words, but usually behaviors work best.

3. These ideas are important to develop a mental construct or a solid template of what "right looks like." It is at these moments that we can really learn because we know what alternative options look like. If your dad was Jeffrey Dahmer then he might struggle with teaching you what 'right looks like.'

4. One of the key aspects of Fromm's theory is that the mother and father balance each other out by providing conditional and unconditional love. It is the Ying/Yang of Love.

CHAPTER 8

Okay fine, maybe it's both of us...

This is the part of the book that we realize that nothing can be all the other person yet it cannot be all you. (I apologize to all those controlling type A people, I normally wouldn't apologize, but if I don't you'll find some way to make it 'your fault' and torture yourself for weeks to come.) This is the part of the book where we learn some balance to the system. Nothing can ever be owned by only one entity or person.

All of us at one time or another find ways to focus our time and attention to elements or aspects that we have absolutely no influence over. This is an interesting concept within itself. We expel energy into something where we cannot reap any reward. It is likely a first world phenomenon, but regardless, it plagues so many people. In the last six years I have seen this issue present itself in politics and world affairs. People become entrenched in a political debate, or ethical item and throw themselves head first into the abyss. The outcome tends to be feeling powerless over their world and fixating on those items. The way to move through the anxiety is to examine this concept:

1.) Circle of Influence/ Circle of Concern/Circle of behavior

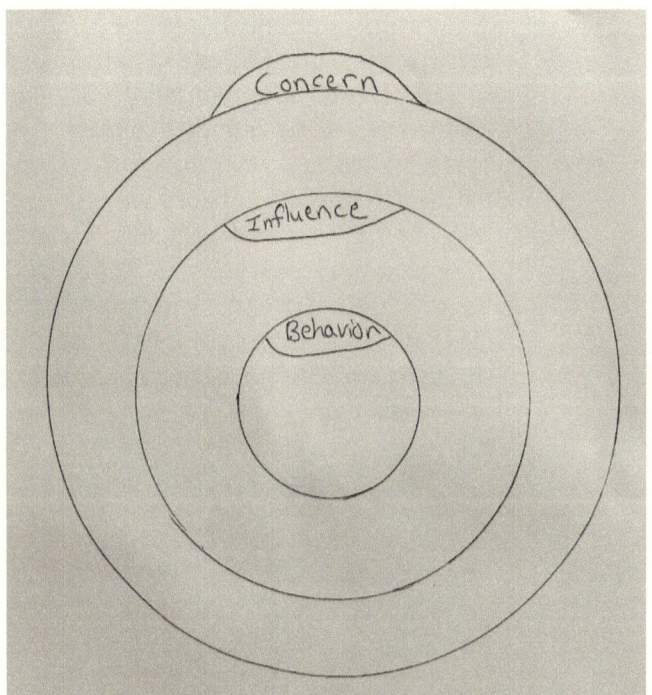

a.

b. If you take time and look at the image you will see three circles. I want to draw your attention to the larger circle first (then move inwards). The outer circle are the things that you cannot control but bother you. It could be your aunt Matilda's wart growing not one but two hairs. If this concerned you greatly you would place this in the outer circle. The circle of influence would include ways you can possibly influence the situation. Remember in the circle of influence that it is hard to motivate our best friends at times, so this circle requires careful consideration. Maybe for Matilda you could influence her by inviting a well-known waxer to a social party. Maybe talk about ways that you manicure your facial hair or even play a commercial on ways to manage hair growth in undesirable areas. The last circle is the focus on behavior. This behavior is no other than your own. In this example you would spend more energy taking care of your own face and discussing teaching facial hair growth to your children and close friends.

i. A more serious example would be A) Circle of concern: Starving children in a foreign country B) Donate money to well researched organizations or finding a group that works directly with that country to provide food or medical aid. It could include donating your own time to travel to that location for a week or two in order to help. It could even be developing a social media group to increase awareness and later help support. Whatever the solution, it is one that you can and will fit into your life on a small or large scale. Last (behavior), you follow through with what you decided to do with consistency and timeliness.

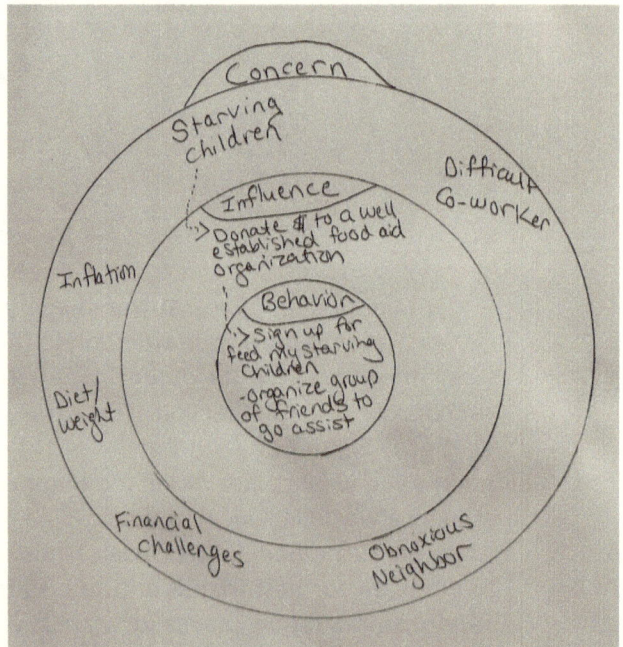

ii.

iii. Remember the focus of this exercise is that if we spend time (which I usually equate to money) then we spend money on things that will not develop a return on investment. We want to spend money (time/energy) on things that make us feel better and more committed to those around us.

2.) Levels of development – where are you... why is this important

    a. This next concept is used mostly when you feel as if you don't understand where someone else is coming from or they don't understand you. When we want to understand other people's behavior it is important to have a framework for judgment (oops) I mean understanding. None of us judge others, not even that shit driver we were stuck behind yesterday (whoops) just kidding. Where was I? Oh yes, understanding dumb drivers, I mean other people.

        i. Part of the framework rests in understanding that there are multiple concepts and theories on human development. In fact, I spent an entire semester in graduate school understanding that complexity. There is one theory that helps organize human behavior in a more clean and organized manner. We are going to call this the three tiers of development.

            1.) The first layer is dependence. One must go through dependence to arrive at the next phase. The challenge is that in this phase you rely on others to help with all your basic needs in the early years. It means that most likely your parents or caregiver ensures that you're fed and sheltered, with clothes and access to medical care. In this phase your needs and wants emotionally and physically are being provided by someone other than yourself. If you grow out of this, then you typically move out in your late teens. If you stay in this phase as an adult, you will see parasitic behaviors. These people tend to depend on others for financial support (it could be family, friends, or gov't. etc.) and they are also not responsible for their behavior, especially if they do something wrong. Taking responsibility is not gonna happen. You have a better chance of getting a germaphobe to lick a urinal at a truckstop than getting a dependent phase person to admit fault, take blame, then take action.

....

2.) The second layer is independence. This is for people that transfer out of dependence, not everyone moves into this phase. During independence the individual owns their behavior and becomes financially independent. People in this phase tend to have a great deal of pride for transferring out of the dependent phase, they tend to view this transition as a rite of passage.

   a. The challenge in this phase is that a lot of people tend to become so prideful of their new-found independence that they look at those still in dependence with disdain.

   b. The other issue is that oftentimes people are so proud of this freedom that they will focus on always being independent. These individuals can often embody that old parable: 'Cut off your nose to spite your face.'

   c. Another obstacle in this phase is trying to be in such control that you overextend your actual abilities, taking on a type of superhero perspective. It is an illusion, almost as impressive as the 'sawing a woman in half' routine put on by magicians.

   d. The problem is that if you constantly tell others that, "you don't need them" then it only takes so long before those around you start to believe that sentiment. We don't want to send the message that we don't need others. Be careful... because people can only hear, "I don't need you, I can do this by myself" so many times until they believe the message you are sending.

   e. Keep in mind that all of us want to be desired, loved, appreciated, and included. Independent people tend to enjoy helping others and will even say, "I like lending a hand to others, I just hate asking for help." This phrase is contradictory.

....

We can't enjoy giving and refuse to take, that will create an imbalance. The worse component is that if you only give and never take then you are stripping the ones you love of the opportunity to feel value and contributing to the betterment of your life.

 f. Independence is important, self-sufficiency is important, but not at the expense of your loved one's sense of value and contribution.

3.) The last phase, and the hardest and fewest number of people is: Interdependency. This phase is when you shift into a type of fluid movement from phase one and two. This is the sweet spot, the 'money maker as they say in the business.' (I'm not sure what business, but I do know that's what they say, and I'm really unclear of 'who' they are, but they sure do sound like they know something.)

 a. Key elements in this phase rest in the adoption of being humble. One does not need to boast to everyone that they make money, are financially independent, and own all of their behavior and manage their emotions.

 b. To live in this phase one would ask for help and support when they damn well know that they do not 'need' it. This creates a more fluid, give and take organization. The focus of this section is also on contribution into one's community. This is a focus on bettering others and more self-lessness.

 c. As stated earlier, this is rarely achieved because there are so many areas that get in the way and inhibit this achievement from taking place. Interdependency means being a 'team player.'

    d. Understanding these different phases is important because it will help you understand others. It will help you organize your own thoughts and develop ways to achieve your goals. Change requires insight and this is a great tool to help increase your awareness and the awareness of others.

3.) Expectations – scales vs. seesaw.

    a. This section is tricky. It is important to understand that people have expectations of others all the time. Being biased can even fall under the umbrella of Expectations. One person believes that another person is going to engage in a set fashion.

    b. This concept is very dangerous in relationships, especially intimate ones. The concern is that some people operate from such a routine script that fights/disagreements can break out even with a sigh from one party. Those non-verbal sound effects can even pack an emotional punch. The smallest form of communication becomes blown up and exaggerated. "INCOMING, INCOMING, INCOMING, DUCK FOR COVER." Well, at least that's how some arguments feel after one word or the sound effects.

    1.) Let us jump into a few pitfalls with the way we develop our expectations. If we go back to the beginning we can see that the average 0-5 year old develops memories, even if those memories are not able to be recalled until the age of 5+. Those experiences are focused into competition of : Time – Attention – Toys → who dictates the winner? (Parents)

        a. Now in elementary school the competition is for : Time – Attention – Grades and who dictates the lead? → Teachers

        b. If you're in athletics you compete for: Playing Time – Scoring – Attention and who dictates the winner? → Coach

c. Once one enters the work force they are in competition at their job for: Hours – Promotion – Accolades and who dictates the top? → Boss

   i.   After we look at these sections 1) Childhood 2) Education 3) Athletics and 4) Job/career there are two common elements of all life experiences = Competition and 3rd Party decider (authoritarian party)

   ii. Now... Here comes the challenge to enter an intimate relationship that is not conducive for an environment of competition and since there are only two people, it does not warrant having a 3rd party decider. In partnerships, the quickest way to make a relationship go rotten is to compete and bring other people into the relationship to judge which one is right. Those two ingredients leave a relationship recipe for disaster.

   iii. Relationships that get stuck on competition have 2 different things that happen. Most relationships that compete will keep what I call a tally system. This is when each person's contribution is measured. For example, "I did the dishes the last two days. I worked 5 extra hours this week, we ate where you wanted to the last three times." I think you get the picture. The second part is that when people compete they also argue over who is 'right'. This is a great way to have a relationship crash and burn.

   iv. The problem with 'being right,' is that it means that someone has to be 'wrong.' The difficulty with that set up is that nobody enjoys being wrong. Raise your hand if you enjoy being wrong and being 'shown up.' (Google has ruined some time-honored fights that could never be resolved until someone went to the library, so Google has added an express lane to the 'you are wrong according to this source.') The other difficulty in being right is that you will sit on your 'throne of rightness' all by yourself because nobody will want to be in your kingdom.

v. Remember this phrase, memorize it, get it tattooed on your forearm, "Would you rather be right or would you rather get along? Because you cannot do both."

vi. This next part will definitely lose me any brownie points I've scored, but please, do not shoot the messenger. Here we go, "Life is not fair, it will never be fair or equal." This comes into play for a number of reasons, but the key component is that people walk into marriages or long term relationships with an erroneous concept that there is a system of fairness and equality. When I give a lecture on this topic I talk about a few items. 1) Remember those traditional wedding vows, "In sickness and in health." In the class I find someone who's married and I ask, "When you gave your wedding vows did you agree upon how many sick days you each would get a year?" This usually gets me a few laughs, but more importantly, a few light bulbs. I go on to ask the audience. 'Think about childbirth. In a heterosexual relationship is there anything a man can do that is fair and equal to the process of making a baby, carrying it in you for 9 months, giving birth, then feeding it with your milk? Is there a set number of income, or is it like 100,00 dishes and 44,000 utensils? We can see how there is nothing that would be fair/equal.

vii. The key component is the need to shift into a teamwork approach. Think of it as a team playing soccer. You have never seen a player get close to the goalie and stop mid play and say, "Hey, I've kicked the ball 5x today and Glen only kicked it 3x so far. That's not fair, I'm not going to kick this opportunity in front of me." If we are a team we just work together. We don't keep track and we just support one another.

    viii. The objective is to shift from I/Me to Us/We and make a cognitive choice regularly to put the partnership above the individual.

2.) Power of touch – This segment is dedicated to the monkeys that underwent the Harlow monkey research project (so sorry baby monkeys). The moral of this story is that humans (and monkeys) need to be comforted (loved) above the need for food. Keep in mind that this study wouldn't happen today, even if it provided a solid understanding of basic needs versus wants.

    a. In the study they took newborn monkeys away from the mother and provided it with two options. A wire "mother" that held mother's milk. Or a 'mother' that was a cylinder with carpet wrapped around it. Then the researchers would present a loud noise and the monkey always ran to the soft mother, not the one that provided food, but rather the emotional connection.

    b. It's important to keep in mind that the baby went to the soft version, which also lets us know that even as adults in our most vulnerable place… we need to feel accepted and loved. We need physical affection. Hugging or being held is a great way to meet this need. Remember that hugs lasting longer than 30 seconds can decrease our cortisol levels therefore decreasing our stress levels.

    c. People (ah-hem… throat clearing) you, (cough again) need to feel valued in order to feel a greater sense of love.

CHAPTER 9

Shit, maybe it's ALL of us....

1.) While it would be nice to place all responsibility (blame) on one person, it is also not very realistic. The challenge is that when we are in a group, other people might pull out different interactions and behaviors. Think back to the class clown (unless it was you and then shame on you for distracting those other students). When the class clown was on a roll you felt inclined to join in, or laugh, but if everyone else wasn't laughing then you became annoyed with the class clown. This is where group dynamics plays an enormous role.

   a. It is important to understand that when four or more people get together that a dynamic will always occur. Basically, there are four roles/jobs that take place. It happens every time. In this section we will just kiss the surface. This entire concept is a full class so there is a lot of content. The purpose right now is to increase the basic understanding so that you can realize that many interactions have nothing to do with you, but rather are nested in biological human dynamics that have been in place for thousands of years. (See, it's not you, but it is you... hmm that's confusing).

   b. Let's take a closer look at each of the players. The first role is that of the Group Leader. This is the person that oversees the others. This person can be picked by the group members, or is assigned by someone outside the group. For example, when you start working at a job the manager is already there, someone else picked them. When you hang out with friends one person tends to take charge and they are in control of the plans or organizing events.

i.   The role of the Group Leader is to establish the rules and consequences/rewards. They must remain consistent and cannot have favorites. Their job is to remain predictable and inclusive of everyone in the group. They are not fully accepted into the group until everyone agrees to follow the Group Leader. The group members *'Have'* to… but they must *'Want'* to…follow the group leader. This may include an act where the team believes that the Group Leader has as much to lose as the members. The team needs to believe that the Group Leader is invested.

ii.   The next leader is the Emotional Leader. This person can interact and communicate with everyone on the team. This is the human glue. They are the person that pulls in each key leader and keeps the harmony in the group. It is the Emotional Leader's responsibility to reach out to the Defiant and Scapegoat Leader (Yes, now you are introduced to the upcoming next Leaders).

iii.   Then we have the Defiant Leader. This is the one that you need and might even enjoy most of the time even though the Group Leader likes them the least. The Defiant Leader's job is to test the sincerity and consistency of the Group Leader. They are the loudest voice if any injustice takes place. The Defiant will test all of the rules or boundaries established by the Group Leader to see if each of the rules will be upheld and how they will be endorsed. If you are not the Group Leader you tend to like this person because they say what everyone else is thinking and typically piss off the boss.

iv.   Last is the Scapegoat Leader. This is the role where everyone likes to dislike you. This is the person that you find yourself saying, "If _____ would just leave, this would be a great place to work." Or you might say, "If _____ would go away this would be a fun activity. The problem with this sentiment is that if you don't pull the Scapegoat into the group, then a new Scapegoat will emerge. It's important to understand that the Scapegoat Leader possesses something in the group. They represent a quality or characteristic that the other members dislike. This trait is usually something that the members fear. It may be a quality that they truly fear that they actually possess. You will find that if you dislike the 'lazy' person in the group it's because you secretly fear being perceived as lazy yourself.

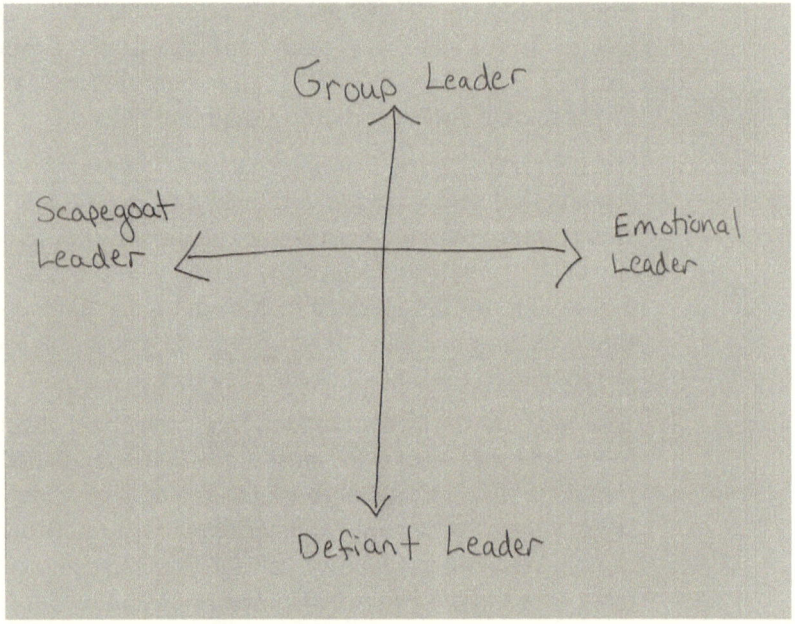

1.) Now that we have the key players identified, it may be important to be aware that if the group is big enough, then co-leaders will emerge.

2.) There are phases of the group and it is important to take a 'pulse' on the temperament of the group.

    a.   The first phase identifies the 'What is the goal?' For people to be in a group they must first come to a consensus that this 'thing' is a shared goal with everyone in the group. Many people agree to this, but usually get stuck on the next phase, the 'how' component.

    b.   The next place a lot of people get stuck is the 'how' the goal is going to be completed. Those in the group can agree on a mission but differ on the How they will make that happen. The how is like the mathematical equation. There are many ways to get to the ultimate goal, but it's hard to get everyone to agree.

    i.   So now picture you are happy and skipping and gleefully in love. You both decide to get married because you have a shared goal... Live happily ever after.

    ii.   Now, you agreed on the goal, but you did not agree on the how? The 'how' is the method in which the primary goal is achieved. This is where one of the partners may believe that their 'happily ever after' involves traveling the country being nomadic. The other partner may believe their 'happily ever after' is settling down in a small town and having 2.5 children and a dog. The 'How' is drastically different. People tend to stop communicating after the goal is established.

    iii.   In group dynamics the group has to agree on the how (at least the four group leaders).

    iv   Interestingly enough, these first two phases are what most couples error on and this frequently leads to divorce. (This is because in a marriage over time the united goal and the how to get there changes so much.)

c.   The next objective/phase is for the Group Leader to pull the Emotional Leader into the group. This takes place when the Emotional Leader agrees to be aligned and assist the Group Leader on the how of the goal.

d.   Then, phase four is when the Emotional Leader pulls in the Defiant Leader and closely after the Group Leader also pulls in the Defiant leader.

e.   After that, the Emotional Leader will pull in the Scapegoat Leader. Shortly after the Group Leader will pull them in and lastly the Defiant Leader will also accept the Scapegoat Leader into the group.

f. After everyone is pulled into the group, the group is now a cohesive well-oiled machine. The co-leaders are also pulled into the group. This is typically because the Mission/Objective remains so well defined.

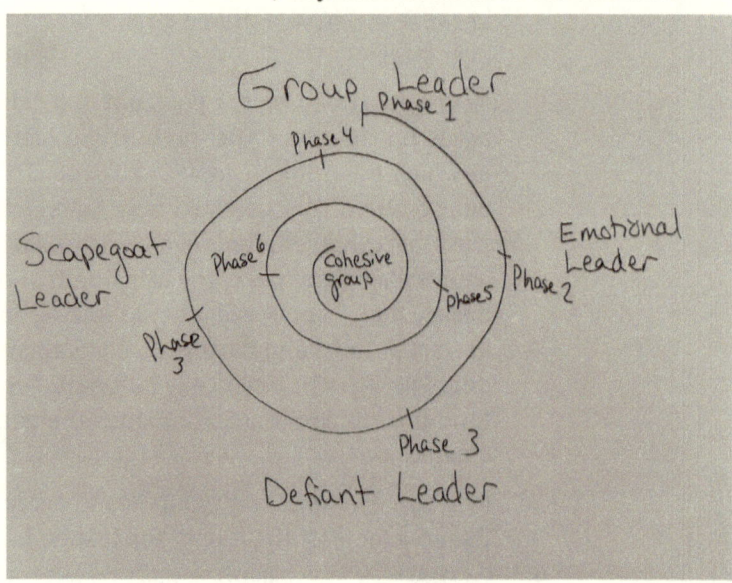

c. Don't take it personal – It is easy to believe that we are all really three years old again and the world revolves around us. The challenge is that we are not really that important. Sometimes when people are mean or rude or disrespectful it has nothing to do with you, it might just be a projection of their own insecurity or challenge. There are many people in the world that are bad listeners. They struggle with never feeling heard and ironically, in turn they don't put in the effort to listen to others. There is an eloquent phrase, "You have two ears and one mouth, everything should be proportional to that equation." What that means is, listen twice as much as you speak. (Thank you Dr. Dodzik)

CHAPTER 10

Can I just eat my feelings….

1.) All of us have developed ways to manage our emotions, or more accurately mis-manage our emotions. Sometimes we get it right and often we make several mistakes before we hit the sweet spot. One of the most common reactions to emotions is to fill the emptiness with food. It makes sense, I'm feeling a deficit and I need to fill it. Why, there is that delicious item that when every time I eat it, I receive a huge dopamine dump. Oh those yummy dopamine receptors eliminate my negative feelings for a solid 2 minutes, it's so worth the high…. NOT. Shortly after that buzz, we receive a swift and uninvited visitor, that unwanted guest is guilt. The guilt that follows tends to erase all the fun of that dopamine dump. (Geez, how do we not invite that guy to the party?)

2.) This topic alone has hundreds of books and ideas and plans for how to modify that behavior and eliminate the feelings of guilt. Take a moment and think about the way you eat, when you eat emotionally. For most people they eat high amounts in a short amount of time.

   a. Let me create an image that will use a defibrillator and 'shock' your sensitive nature. The way we eat when feeling highly emotional looks abrasive and has more of a 'animalistic fucking' energy connected. Shift from aggressive eating to making love to your food. The term fucking creates a crass and aggressive visual. There is no love or compassion with that approach. We need to take that concept and move into making sweet sweet love to your food. If we need that dopamine dump, let's remove the guilt and still enjoy the experience. If you know you are still going to eat that 'impulsive' then allow yourself to enjoy the food. Turn on some good music, turn down the lights, light a candle and slow down the speed and amount of which you eat. The idea is that you take smaller bites, enjoy the texture, cherish the taste. Really enjoy the choices that you are making, remove the guilt. Or at least find a way to widdle it down to a manageable dose of anxiety.

CHAPTER 11

Nevermind, can't I just sleep through my life?

1.) Sleep – it's one of the four basic components of a healthy life (The others are a balanced diet/hydration, exercise, and purpose.) Nothing else works if you don't have those addressed.

2.) Sleep is becoming an increasingly difficult item to manage. The amount of Americans with sleep disorders has been on a steady rise for some time. Let's review a few items that might help with just the basics.

    a. The first thing to try is to cover the eyes. I recommend a small t-shirt. Something that is light and can be draped across the face. The luxury of a shirt is that it will fall down next to your nose allowing a full blackout. The trick to covering the eyes is that there cannot be any light. This helps signal to the circadian rhythm rods that it's time to sleep.

        i. There are many discussions about why this is such an issue. A lot of the concerns talk about light pollution. Light pollution is when there's a street light, a television, a charger light, and so on and so forth. These things cause the Theta Wave in your brain to stay engaged because it believes that something is moving or happening in your room.

            1. It is important to remember that the eyes have two functions the same way the ears have two functions. The ears hear and control balance. The eyes control vision and the sleep cycle. If

the eyes register lights or movements, it will tell your brain to 'be on alert.'

b. Shut down the brain – by outsmarting the amygdala. This next one sounds so easy it is almost unbelievable, but first let's get some context.

   i. There are essentially two brains in your head (for my neurogeeks, shhh). There is the old system and the new system. The old system is essentially in a time warp. The old part is trapped in the land of being a caveman. Now while the outfits were probably more comfortable than panty hose and high heels, it left the fashion industry lacking. The old part is still in a constant battle of fight or flight daily. It is always on the hunt for dangers (real or perceived). This part of the brain is the amygdala. Amygdala is Latin for almond. So these little parts look like almonds in your mid brain. You have two of them. Without them you would arguably die. The challenge for the Amygdala is that it only has one job and it takes this job seriously. It's job is to keep you hypervigilant and alive. This system doesn't care if you are embarrassed or if you stay up all night wringing your hands with anxiety. It's probably as close to an unfeeling robot as you can become. 'Must keep you alive, be bo be bop.'

   ii. The other part of your brain (I'm aware of the oversimplification) is your prefrontal lobe. Now this is the sexy and sophisticated part. This is the part where you can hear 'bam bampa bum' while walking in those stockings and high heels. This is where "YOUR" personality lives. This is where your life experiences, your temperament, your successes, your failures, your dreams, all those fun things get filed. This prefrontal lobe wants some damn sleep.

   iii. So... this is the trick. When you're up and your mind is racing, you might be thinking about a sports team, remembering to file your taxes (gross), or wondering if you left the stove on, asking yourself, why did I watch that horror movie about... Once your mind is racing you need to get a piece of paper and a pen/pencil (dealers choice). Lay down in your bed and start writing all the things you need to do. I recommend in a bullet point fashion:

-pick up dog from groomers

-why is my coworker so unreasonable

-gift for my friend's birthday in 2 weeks

-gas for car

-produce for dinner

iv. The first night you do this it can take a while, it may take 20 to 45 minutes. But once you're done your amygdala will quiet down. This is what happens from a neurogeek perspective. The brain is anxious that you have uncompleted tasks. It views these tasks the same as a life-or-death situation. Picking up the dog and getting lettuce for dinner are life threatening items because they create tension or anxiety in the body. When you write things down, the caveman brain interprets this as 'action.' The brain feels a sense of relief and now you can start counting sheep.

c. Organize the room – decrease Theta wave items. Rooms signify behavior or actions. One does not go into the bathroom to make dinner (unless you are a hoarder and can't access your kitchen sink. In any case you'll buy the book but never read it, so it's a wash).

i. The brain identifies rooms with activities. It sees the bathroom as a place of personal hygiene, whether it is voiding or cleaning. It sees the kitchen as a place to prepare food or eat. The dining room for eating or socializing, playing card/board games. The living room for television or conversation. The bedroom is a place to sleep or have sex. If one places a television and a computer or other stimulating items in the bedroom the brain becomes confused about the task at hand. The standard rule is no electronics in the bedroom. If you have a television in the bedroom, then you can only watch pornography on that television. The brain needs to have clear parameters to operate. Make sure your space is well organized (i.e., get rid of electronics in your bedroom. If I wasn't clear, anything that plugs in or needs to be charged, other than a vibrator, it does not belong in your bedroom).

d. Dreams – what do they mean – why am I killing everyone?

  i. There are many debates about dreams and many books that have an opinion on dreams. The ones that I've found to be the most organized and the most helpful say that dreams are an access to our subconscious. Neuroscience argues that dreams are consciousness since we can recall the dream and we have feelings while in the dream.

  ii. What I have found interesting in my work with dreams is how very personal the dreams feel to the individual. Many people will share a dream but feel embarrassed or vulnerable by sharing the dream. It's important to remember a few basic rules about dreams.

     1.) Every person in the dream is an aspect of yourself. For example: if your boss is in the dream, then when you wake up, write down 3 adjectives about the person/boss. Maybe the adjectives are 1) demanding 2) selfish 3) small-minded. Then the dream is about the ways that you are being demanding/selfish/small-minded.

     2.) When you wake up, finish the dream if it's stressful. If in the dream you are lost and can't get to your destination, then when you wake up picture yourself arriving. This will help you better navigate your dreams and help you feel more empowered. When you can take charge of your dreams, you can become more in control of your subconscious drives.

3.) Ask yourself for guidance. If there is a big decision to be made or something on your mind, ask yourself for the answer before you go to bed at night. For example, "Should I switch jobs?" While you are sleeping your subconscious will begin to answer you.

CHAPTER 12

I'm just depressed.... (I tried to have a funnier title, but I was too depressed to think of one)

1.) A plan – having a plan to manage your depression will always help.

    a. Anticipated Shifts – calendar – identifying patterns. As we grow older, we tend to have a better understanding of our strengths and weaknesses. Part of knowing our limits involves understanding if there are times of the year it is more difficult than others.

        i. I have noticed over the years that everyone gets depressed in September. As we look at that month it symbolizes a time of change. Typically, every September, from the time memory consolidation takes place (age 5), you started something new in September. There would be a new school year, with new teachers/students. It was a time of transition. If you are a parent, now your children are experiencing that change.

        ii. Identify if you have a death or a traumatic experience anniversary. Many times our brain will make connections to events and lock them in with dates. (Psst, there are ways to stop this phenomena) In the meantime, awareness is the key to addressing these underlying items.

        iii. The trick is to be aware of these shifts so that one can preplan. The goal is to not be 'caught off-guard' and have a plan on how to address these emotional shifts before they are sitting on your doorstep.

b. Environmental stressors – accumulation effect

   i. Ahh, the dangerous accumulation effect, the proverbial quote, "the straw that broke the camel's back." That proverb was created to let everyone have a limit. You may be close to your own limit.

   ii. The main way to view this challenge rests in the idea of examining events occurring around you. There is a great question to ask yourself, "Would this have bothered me two weeks ago?" If the answer is 'no' then you are feeling stressed due to an accumulation effect (too much shit on your plate). If you ask the question, "would this have bothered me two weeks ago?" and the answer is 'yes' then you know that the situation is very upsetting and probably needs to be addressed.

   iii. If there are no external issues then you know that something hormonally might be off. (It's usually at this point that you might want to see a psychiatrist).

c. Push down the boulder – this next one is a great visualization, but it needs to have the follow through in actions to work the best. Imagine depression as a large boulder on the top of a steep hill. Most people will get in front of the boulder and try to push it back up, but that never works. Gravity has a thing to say and the boulder eventually heads down the hill and crushes you in the meantime leaving you squished and drained. Afterwards it takes you weeks to recuperate. Imagine instead that you either push the boulder down yourself to speed up the process, or start running down the hill and remove all potential obstacles in your way. If you push it down or remove obstacles then you 1) don't get squished 2) have more energy once the boulder is down the hill.

   i. What most people do when they are becoming depressed is fight the depression. When you feel that nagging heavy feeling most people will spend their energy pushing it away or ignoring it. What happens is that if you push it away it eventually overtakes you. The problem with 'fighting off' your depression is that you waste energy. If you spend (what little energy you have) fighting against yourself then soon you are drained. There is nothing left in the tank and there are no reserves.

ii.   What do you look like in your worst depression? Are you isolating? Eating ice cream? Watching movies? Playing games? Listening to music? Identify what actions you take. Once you have those identified (maybe make a list) then when you feel a depressive episode coming on, immediately take the time off of work/school/life and perform the activities you need to fill you back up. Why wait until you are totally drained and squished? So, pushing the boulder means you take time off right away and figure out your self-soothing techniques. Removing obstacles means that maybe in a few days (after a big project) you take the time to yourself.

iii.   The maximum timeline is 24-48 hours – this will prevent the two-week time frame of a typical depressive episode (for hormones to be replenished). The challenge with depression is that it is cyclical. Meaning once you are in a depressive episode it can be hard to shift gears. I often imagine a train. Once the train stops moving it takes a great amount of energy to get it going again. If the train just slows down, then it's easier to get it back up to the ideal speed.

iv.   After your timeline expires (24-48 hours) you need to return to work and your routines. Routine is what will keep you on track and stabilized. Structure is what helps our brain feel organized.

Making plans is a good way to help decrease anxiety and feel like you are in control of your life, but always remember, you can make a plan while God says, "Hold my beer!"

CHAPTER 13

I'm having a panic attack over my depression...
WHAT?

1.) Anxiety and Depression as glasses of water

    a. The first thing you need to identify is your core disposition. Are you primarily a depressed person or an anxious person? Everyone leans more heavily to one side. This is how you view the world. Do you spend most of your time being reflexive (looking backwards) or worrying about the future (looking forwards)?

    b. Now that you have your 'core' response, think of each emotion: depression and anxiety as 2 empty glasses (one for each). As time and life experiences occur, your primary emotion cup gets filled up. It may get filled halfway, then up and down over time. When too many stressful events occur (back to that damn straw and camel thing) the glass will become full. Once the glass is full, it cannot overflow, it must be poured into the other glass. It is at this moment, when one glass gets poured into another, that you believe that you have 'gone crazy'. You have not in fact 'gone crazy' but rather you are experiencing an emotion that is ingenuine to yourself. If you are normally an anxious person and your anxiety glass becomes full you will become depressed. This feeling is new and uncomfortable and frankly, scary. Your thoughts aren't organized in the same pattern as they are used to, and you don't like it.

c. Remember that when the glass tips over, it is temporary. Determine if there are things you can remove from your plate. Find ways to lean into your support system. Take a day to yourself. Whatever it is, your body will find the homeostasis again, it will just take a bit of time.

d. Lastly, remember that if you 'think you're going crazy', that you cannot in fact be crazy. (Also remember that crazy is a cultural term and not a medical/clinical term, so it doesn't actually exist.) But if you feel like you are not in your right mind, those people that suffer from schizophrenia and delusions believe that everyone else is 'crazy' and they are the only sane people. So, if you fear that you are 'going crazy' then you in fact cannot be delusional.

2.) Glass half full/empty – ahh the great debate. Are you a person that sees the glass as half full or half empty. This is a concept that has plagued many people over many decades.

a. Here is the puzzle, a glass is filled halfway with water (or Jack Daniels or lemonade, whatever your poison). Are you a person that sees the glass as half-full or half-empty? This question is supposed to determine if you are an optimist or pessimistic person, but if you're pessimistic you really consider yourself a realist. I challenge you to see this in another fashion.

b. For a number of years I had a therapy dog that worked with me. Her name was Riley and she was trained at one of the prisons I worked at. She was the smartest dog I have ever met. (She was actually smarter than me, which makes behavioral training a bitch haha pun intended). Well, she was so smart that she would become depressed at times, especially when she knew she wasn't getting what she wanted. She would mope and sulk around the house. At the same time, I also had a puppy mill rescue dog Spot. Spot was clearly inbred and the happiest dog in the world. She never had a bad emotion or day. She was also not burdened by intelligence. A nine-year-old boy once said, "When Riley looks at a glass filled half-way depending on her mood she will see it as half-full or half-empty. But when Spot looks at the glass she says, "Let's Drink."

i. Sometimes in life we need to think, "Let's drink." It often does not benefit us to spend time and energy debating on the fullness of the glass. We should rather stay in the moment and enjoy what's in front of us.

3.) The smoke detector for the brain is the amygdala. It alerts us to problems. Anxiety is the physical sensation to let us know that something is going on. Anxiety is the indicator. When you are feeling anxious, that is the time that you need to gather more information. It is a good thing when you're anxious. It means that you need to make a list of questions. After you have the list, then identify where you can get them answered. After you've gathered all the information, then you can decide. A well-educated decision.

4.) The next best thing to do in order to manage anxiety is exercise. I know I know. That sounds horrible. The only way to decrease cortisol levels (stress hormones) is through exercise, having a heart rate over 120 for at least 20 minutes a day. Stress can also create more fat cells. This means that we can decrease anxiety (fat) by exercising regularly and keeping our negative hormone levels at a safe place. This doesn't mean that you have to get a gym membership and dedicate 2 hours a day (although I would not discourage that) but rather, put on a backpack and go for a brisk walk, 10 min out and 10 min back. Your heart and your body will love you more for this decision.

CHAPTER 14

MOMMMM, My partner/coworker/friend won't get along with me....

1.) Miscommunication = likely the oldest story in mankind. Most issues in your life are a result of miscommunication. Either in what you said vs what you intended and the same goes for the other person, what they said versus what they intended.

2.) This next section is the WTF in communication. So, if you find yourself thinking, "What the Fuck did you just say?", then you automatically know that miscommunication took place. Rarely does anyone, friend, family, coworker, associate say something purposely offensive (unless you are on social media, then all rules are off). For those people that know you, they don't want to hurt you, but often it's those we know best that say the most cutting of words.

3.) So, when you find yourself thinking, "What the F*&% did you say?" Then you know 1) miscommunication has taken place 2) You need to ask clarifying questions. 3) Keep asking questions until you have a clearer understanding. It is important that when you ask the questions, if you're not gaining any traction in the conversation then you need to share the emotions that are being evoked. It may look like this, "I'm feeling vulnerable with what you just said." Or whatever emotion you are experiencing.

   a. Here's an example. I had a client who had a newborn. She was having a hard time pumping and breastfeeding. She continued to internally question her production of milk and at times they needed to supplement her breast milk. At month five she heard her husband in the kitchen say, "Well I guess I need to get milk." She thought, "WTF did you say?" She was immediately upset with him. When he said that he needed to get milk she had interpreted that as she wasn't making enough breast milk. She activated the WTF and said, "What do you mean you need to get milk? I'm feeling like a bad mother by not making enough milk." He responded with, "I wasn't talking to you honey, I was making my grocery list, I also need to get eggs and toilet paper. You're a wonderful mother. Why are you feeling bad?"

b. See how clearly this conversation was explained. It took just a few clarifying statements. Of course, the clarification only occurred because one person was willing to be vulnerable and ask supporting questions.

c. The next important question to ask yourself is, "Would I rather be right or get along?"

d. The problem with being right is that it means that someone else is wrong. Nobody wants to be wrong. So, if you're trying to get along with someone else, then if you point out how wrong the other person is, they are unlikely to see your perspective (I'm being polite, they will not see your side and in fact become pissed at you). The problem with being right is that you will sit alone on your 'throne of rightness' all by yourself. Nobody will want to be in your kingdom.

e. Always remember... "Do I want to be right or get along?" I hope that you pick 'get along.'

CHAPTER 15

Should I stay or should I go now.... If I go there will be trouble, if I stay it will be double (in the words of the clash)

I. Double pro/con list

    A. This section is about major life decisions. We are all faced with them and it can be oh so tricky to figure out. The key to this one is closely tied to the idea of a pro/con list. But this is actually called a 'double pro/con list.' A typical pro/con list just has the decision that needs to be made and pro's and con's. This leaves too many other variables out of the equation and people still tend to feel crippled in making a decision. In the double pro/con list we list out both potential outcomes. Let's say you're debating getting a dog. There would be four columns. The first thing would be 'Get a Puppy' and underneath would be a pro/con list. Then next to it would be 'Don't get a Puppy' with a pro/con list underneath.

    B. List all of the concerns/issues/thoughts related to getting a puppy or not getting a puppy. Many items will show up twice, but you will see that they may hold different values.

    C. Next you will write down the emotional/energy value you place on each item. It can have values from 1 to 100. Remember it is the absolute value. So if the idea of picking up dog poop on a soggy spring day creates an upsetting image it may be worth 60 to you, even if it feels like a negative.

D. Now, on rare occasions you can have something valued at higher than 100, but it can only be once and I usually discourage it, because it will throw off the numbers quickly. But there are times that it is rated higher than 100.

E. Add up each column. Subtract the cons from the pros. See the total number for each section (Get Puppy/Don't Get Puppy). That is the outcome for the decision.

II. Mentally make a commitment.

A. I see this with large decisions. People will vacillate from one decision to the next and continue to feel 'stuck' on the fence. If one continues to keep looking at both sides of the fence they will tend to feel overwhelmed by the choices.

B. Mentally pick one option. For example; break up with a boyfriend. Maybe you have been going back and forth in your mind for months. This is not helpful. Make a mental decision. For the next one to two weeks picture yourself broken up. See your future apart. Mentally commit and see all the small ways your world would be different. From eating meals to bathroom hygiene to inside jokes. Write down those reactions at the end.

C. Next, pick the other side. Decide to stay together, picture that for one to two weeks. Commit to that decision and see all the ways it would impact you. Remember you can't get mad (be reactive) and think about leaving, you have mentally committed to finding a way to work it out. After the time is up, write down your feelings.

D. Decide if you need to make a decision quickly or if you can gather more information.

E. Typically, after the exercise the decision is clear and your subconscious will help you navigate those waters rapidly without all the extra confusion of the back and forth.

CHAPTER 16

Now a word from my sponsors

1.) Bahaha I don't have any sponsors, but I do have clients that sponsor my love of therapy and being a psychologist.

2.) Per request of one of my clients, they asked me to make a special comment about weaponizing therapy words. I imagine that the phrase will paint a picture or bring you to an experience with someone that was unpleasant.

3.) My first experience with weaponizing therapy words was when I worked in a prison. During group therapy the inmates would become mad at one another and call the other person by their diagnosis. It was so frequent that it became a group rule, "you are not allowed to call anyone else by their diagnosis or you will be kicked out of the group."

4.) One of the most common abuses of psychology words is trigger. I caution people on misuse/abuse of words. If we take words and overuse them, we lose the power. If you are upset, use words to describe the behavior that you don't like.

Lastly, thank you for taking the time out to improve yourself. Remember, it just takes insight and motivation to make change. Hopefully this book has given you some insight. Now you just need to have the motivation.

Yours truly,

Dr. Savage

Final parting thoughts, part for humor, part for reality: Proverb with a twist of my humor...

You can lead a horse to water, but you can't drown it. This one is reserved for the times that you did everything you can for a friend or a loved one and they just won't take your advice or your help, most common with addictions, and now your emotions have turned to rage.

The grass IS greener on the other side of the fence. Well, that is until you jump over the fence, eat all the grass, and shit all over the place. Then it will look like where you just left.

The suggestion of thumb. If you haven't been paying attention to the rule of thumb then you've probably had your thumb up your a$$ and you need to pay attention to the audience around you.

Easy come easy let go. If it came to you easily, then it frequently has lower value. Let go of the little things.

Fortune favors the second bold. Never the first one, that person becomes a scapegoat, but the next person has a chance to run interference.

It is... what you make it. Not it is what it is. If you don't like it... fix it. Don't take the scraps in life.

You can put lipstick on a pig and it still looks better than before the lipstick. Sometimes we just need to shine up that old penny. Or polish that turd.

In for a penny, don't give away any more cash. In for a penny in for a pound is a shitty way to explain the continuous loss of money. Stop wasting your energy or money. No more pennies!

It's only a good story if you get away with it. Move away from 'only illegal if you get caught'. Nope, it's still illegal even if you don't get caught. This is the framework for cognitive dissonance. This is where you talk yourself into bad ideas. Remember, every bad decision will eventually see the light of day. Is this a story you want to tell your kids or grandma?

If you're going to be late, be prepared. If you're going to mess up with time, at least put the effort into knowing what you are walking yourself into! Remember proper planning prevents piss poor performance.

Any port in a storm! This one doesn't need to be updated. It's perfect. Sometimes we are just happy that we are out of that damn storm.

Don't judge a book by it's cover if you can't read good. This one is about how many people pass judgement without the information, but also without an understanding of the information you are receiving. This is sort of like the saying, "I can tell you, but I can't make you understand."

Don't be a Wool blanket. This one is special because people say don't be a wet blanket, but if we are being honest, when things start getting wet that's when the real fun begins (wink emoji) a wool blanket is scratchy and dry and devoid of any kind of fun that could happen. Remember, there is a reason that wool is not part of lingerie. Don't be a wool blanket, devoid of moisture and fun!

References:

Changing for GoodCycle of change, Prochaska & DiClemente printed by Harpers Collins Jan 1994

The Art of Loving, by Erich Fromm printed by Harper Perennial 1956

Happiness Advantage, by Shawn Achor printed by Currency 2018

Group dynamics by Dr. Dugo printed by oxford press 2003

Daz 3D instrument for visual images